AAK-97

WITHDRAWN

HOW TO GET A
JOB
— IN —
EDUCATION

HOW TO GET A
JOB
— IN —
EDUCATION

JOEL LEVIN

Bob Adams, Inc.
Holbrook, Massachusetts

Published by
Bob Adams, Inc.
260 Center Street
Holbrook, Massachusetts

ISBN 0-937860-79-4

Manufactured in the United States of America.

Acknowledgments

I am deeply grateful to the many people who helped make this book a reality: Maxine K. Jacks, Career Counselor/Educational Placement, Office of Career Development and Placement, Northeastern Illinois University, who, along with Dr. Margaret Lindman, Chairperson of the Department of Curriculum and Instruction at the same institution, graciously volunteered time to contribute invaluable research assistance; Ms. Phyllis Henry, Englewood High School, Chicago, and Doctoral Candidate at the University of Illinois at Chicago Circle, who supported this project from its inception and provided much essential material; and John and Tina Lillig, and the staff at Bob Adams Inc., especially Brandon Toropov, who contributed complete cooperation and encouragement. Finally, a very special thank-you goes to my wife Peggy for her tireless efforts and her unending understanding.

This book provides resources for those seeking employment in elementary and secondary education, with special sections on college and university employment and overseas opportunities. While every reasonable effort has been made to obtain accurate information and verify same, occasional errors may result due to the magnitude of the data base. Should you discover an error, please notify the publisher.

CONTENTS

Who This Book Is For

How to Get a Job in Education acquaints thousands of job seekers with the opportunities available to them as teachers in our nation's public elementary and secondary schools.

This book also includes sections on private schools and college and university teaching. It provides a comprehensive overview of the entire job search process in education, from studying for the NTE to applying for an initial teaching certificate; from preparing a resume to contacting local school districts; from making sense out of a contract to undertaking the actual duties of a classroom instructor.

New college graduates who have recently completed teacher training programs, and are beginning their careers as teachers, will find this book an indispensable guide to obtaining that first classroom assignment. Experienced teachers who plan on transferring to a different school district (or simply moving up the education career ladder), will find vital resources in this volume that will aid their quest for a new position. In addition, adults with a four-year college degree in a field other than education, and who are contemplating a career change, will benefit from this book's timely advice on alternative routes to certification, as well as from the overview of the teaching profession as a whole.

INTRODUCTION

These are exciting times to begin your career in education. Not since Sputnik was launched in 1957 has so much attention been focused on our nation's schools. The improvement of America's public school system is in the forefront of media discussion and legislative action. Presidential commissions, state task forces, business and civic groups, and local communities have all voiced their concern over the need to upgrade student achievement and academic standards.

The necessity for competent, dedicated teachers has never been greater than it is today. The oversupply of teaching personnel in the 1970's has been replaced by critical shortages of certified staff. Hiring specialists from local school districts have ventured out of city, out of state, even out of the country in their recruitment efforts.

How to Get a Job in Education will help you join the more than two million elementary and secondary school teachers currently employed in public education. It will prepare you for your job search with realistic, timely advice, and it will guide you through the labyrinth of forms and documents you will encounter on your path to becoming a teacher.

Joel Levin

One:
Facing The Forms

Why Teaching?

Teaching today is one of the best career paths you can follow. Education offers a variety of challenging job opportunities. Some instructors remain in the classroom their entire professional lives, while others move into areas of curriculum writing, achievement testing, special education services, counseling, school administration, or government-mandated programs. Many teachers start at the elementary or secondary school level, but eventually move on to become college professors -- joining almost 700,000 others in our nation's junior colleges, four-year colleges, and universities.

With renewed interest by government leaders in classroom performance, the rewards of teaching have never been greater. Average salaries for public school teachers, according to Education Secretary William J. Bennett, will advance to $28,300 a year. The Carnegie Forum on Education and the Economy, in one of its recent reform proposals, urges a teacher salary norm of $35,000, increasing to $65,000 for lead or master teachers.

In an era of corporate mergers and reorganizations that have sent hundreds of thousands of dedicated and experienced white-collar workers scrambling for new employment, public school teaching offers an island of relative job security. Present and future teacher shortages only portend more job security in coming years.

Winds of change have finally arrived in education. Calls for nationwide teaching standards for certification, restructuring undergraduate education courses, merit pay, master teacher institutes, and competency testing all point in the direction of elevating the professional status of teachers.

Education is an enormous enterprise, one that continues to grow. The government's annual preview of the new school year is highlighted by statistics that show:

*One in every five Americans will be in the classroom.
Public elementary and secondary schools will spend
$168 billion.
Enrollments will total 58 million students.*

Ultimately, however, your choice of teaching as a career rests, not upon statistics, or job security, or salary, but solely upon the satisfaction you derive from the work itself. If you are excited by the possibility of helping children grow and mature into independent, literate adults, you may want to think seriously about entering this challenging -- but highly rewarding -- profession.

Get That State Certificate!

State certification is the key to successfully beginning your job search in education. It is a legal requirement for you to possess and show evidence of an appropriate teaching certificate issued by your State Board of Education. Legally, local school districts may only employ properly certified applicants. Your state certificate (also called a license) should be obtained immediately after college graduation. Delays in being certified or approved for teaching by state officials will bring your job search to an abrupt halt.

Where do you turn first? The answer's fairly simple. Acting as the preliminary screening agency, the State Board of Education (or Department of Public Instruction in some states) must review your qualifications for a teaching position. Contact them immediately and determine whether your college background is suitable for obtaining a certificate. (A listing of all the appropriate boards can be found at the end of this section). If all state guidelines are met, a certificate in your name will be issued. As a certified teacher you may apply to any public elementary or high school district in your state. Graduates of accredited teacher-training programs are, in many cases, entitled to receive a state certificate upon their graduation. However, while these entitlement programs give you the *right* to a teaching certificate, the process of certification is *never* automatic. You must still complete and file the proper application.

Application forms vary to some extent among the 50 states but, generally speaking, be prepared to furnish five basic types of information.

Personal data includes your name, birthdate, permanent address, telephone number and proof of citizenship.

Academic records will highlight the names and dates of all high schools and colleges you have attended and all degrees awarded.

The type of certificate you are seeking will depend upon the area of teaching you wish to enter -- elementary, secondary, special education, etc.

Complete transcripts will outline your educational

background, and are available from your college registrar's office.

Your written account of your experience will detail all previous full-time teaching assignments (not applicable to beginning teachers.)

Many states require a notary public to sign your application for state certification before submission. In completing the application, you should keep several things in mind. Follow all directions carefully. Review each part of the application. Be certain everything is properly completed and legible. Always type or print. (Incomplete or illegible applications will be returned and could cause serious delays in your job search.) Use extra caution now in filing for your teaching certificate so you won't have to make corrections later.

Fees are, of course, required for each certificate and range from $10.00 - $50.00. (Note: sample applications for certification and local school district applications may be found later in this chapter.)

Many teachers qualify for a certificate in more than one education field. Dual certification is valuable and increases your chances for success in the education job market. For example, you may have earned enough college credits to be eligible for an elementary and special education certificate. Applicants possessing state certification in two (or more) areas can, obviously, avail themselves of far greater job opportunities than holders of a single certificate. Each certificate requested requires a separate application, evaluation of your college transcripts and fee.

Don't neglect dual certification even if you are not initially qualified for a second teaching certificate. Enroll in additional courses after graduation. Obtaining a second or third state certificate can be the best professional investment you'll ever make. It will increase your job security and flexibility throughout your entire teaching career.

Update your knowledge of state certification regulations on a periodic basis -- they're constantly changing. (For an in-depth review of the requirements state by state, you may want to consult the appropriate volume of *The Job Bank Guide To Education Employment,* available from this publisher or at your local library). It's your responsibility as an educator to be aware of and fulfill all new requirements in your particular teaching area. Remember: maintaining current state certification is not a one-time procedure;

teaching certificates expire after a given number of years. Be aware of your certificate's date of expiration and take the steps needed for its timely renewal.

State Certification Reciprocity

Many states participate in the Interstate Agreement on Qualifications of Educational Personnel. This compact provides for reciprocity in teacher certification among the member states. For example, if you are certified in one state and then move to a different state, your teaching certificate will still be recognized provided both states are members of the agreement. Of course, it is still your responsibility to submit a formal application in your new state. Research the state regulations thoroughly before you move since certification requirements are constantly changing.

The following states participate in the Interstate Agreement on Qualifications of Educational Personnel:

Alabama	Nebraska
Alaska	New Hampshire
California	New Jersey
Connecticut	New York
Delaware	North Carolina
District of Columbia	Ohio
Florida	Oklahoma
Hawaii	Oregon
Idaho	Pennsylvania
Indiana	Rhode Island
Iowa	South Carolina
Kentucky	South Dakota
Maine	Utah
Maryland	Vermont
Massachusetts	Virginia
Michigan	Washington
Minnesota	West Virginia
Montana	Wisconsin

Addresses of State Teacher Certification Offices

State of Alabama
Department of Education
Teacher Certification Office
349 State Office Building
Montgomery, Alabama 36130
(205)261-5060

State of Alaska
Department of Education
Teacher Certification Office
P.O. Box F
Juneau, Alaska 99811
(907)465-2831

State of Arizona
Department of Education
Teacher Certification Unit
1535 West Jefferson
P.O. Box 25609
Phoenix, Arizona 85002
(602)255-4367

State of Arkansas
Department of Education
Office of Teacher Education,
    Certification, Evaluation
    and Testing
#4 Capitol Mall - Room 107-B
Little Rock, Arkansas 72201-1201
(501)371-1475

State of California
Commission on Teacher
    Credentialing
Licensing Branch
Box 944270
Sacramento, California
    94244-2700
(916) 445-7254

State of Colorado
Department of Education
Teacher Certification
State Office Building
201 East Colfax Avenue
Denver, Colorado 80203
(303)866-6628

State of Connecticut
Department of Education
Teacher Certification Unit
Box 2219
Hartford, Connecticut 06145
(203)566-4561

State of Delaware
Department of Public
    Instruction
Certification and
    Personnel Division
Townsend Building
P.O. Box 1402
Dover, Delaware 19903
(302)736-4686, 87, 88

State of Florida
Department of Education
Teacher Certification Section
Tallahassee, Florida 32301
(904)488-2317

State of Georgia
Department of Education
Teacher Certification Services
Twin Towers East - 1858
Atlanta, Georgia 30334
(404)656-2406

State of Hawaii
Department of Education
Office of Personnel Services
Teacher Certification Unit
P.O. Box 2360
Honolulu, Hawaii 96804
(808)548-5217

State of Idaho
Department of Education
Office of Teacher Certification
Len B. Jordan Building
Boise, Idaho 83720
(208)334-3475

Addresses of State Teacher Certification Offices

State of Illinois
Board of Education
Department of Professional
    Relations
Certification and
    Placement Section
100 North First Street
Springfield, Illinois   62777
(217)782-2805

State of Indiana
Department of Education
Division of Teacher
Education and Certification
Indianapolis, Indiana   46204-2798
(317)232-6636

State of Iowa
Department of Public
    Instruction
Teacher Education and
Certification Division
Grimes State Office Building
Des Moines, Iowa   50319
(515)281-3245

State of Kansas
Department of Education
    Certification,
    Teacher Education,
    Accreditation Section
120 East 10th Street
Topeka, Kansas   66612
(913)296-2288

State of Kentucky
Department of Education
    Bureau of Instruction
Division of Teacher
    Education and Certification
Frankfort, Kentucky   40601
(502)564-4606

State of Louisiana
Department of Education
Bureau of Higher Education
and Teacher Certification
P.O. Box 94064
Baton Rouge, Louisiana
    70804-9064
(504)342-3490

State of Maine
Department of Educational
    and Cultural Services
Teacher Certification/Placement
State House Station 23
Augusta, Maine   04333
(207)289-5945

State of Maryland
Department of Education
Division of Certification
    and Accreditation
200 West Baltimore Street
Baltimore, Maryland
    21201-2595
(301)333-2141, 2143

Commonwealth of
    Massachusetts
Department of Education
Bureau of Teacher Preparation,
Certification and Placement
1385 Hancock Street
Quincy, Massachusetts   02169
(617)770-7517

State of Michigan
Department of Education
Teacher Preparation and
Certification Services
Box 30008
Lansing, Michigan   48909
(517)373-3310

Addresses of State Teacher Certification Offices

State of Minnesota
Department of Education
Personnel Licensing Section
616 Capitol Square
550 Cedar Street
St. Paul, Minnesota 55101
(612)296-2046

State of Mississippi
Department of Education
Division of Instruction
Office of Teacher
Education and Certification
P.O. Box 771
Jackson, Mississippi 39205
(601)359-3483

State of Missouri
Department of Elementary
and Secondary Education
Teacher Education
    and Certification
P.O. Box 480
Jefferson City, Missouri 65102
(314)751-3486

State of Montana
Office of Public Instruction
Division of Certification
and Teacher Education
State Capitol
Helena, Montana 59620
(406)444-3095

State of Nebraska
Department of Education
Office of Teacher Certification
301 Centennial Mall South
Box 94987
Lincoln, Nebraska 68509
(402)471-2496

State of Nevada
Department of Education
State Mail Room
215 E. Bonanza
Las Vegas, Nevada 89158
(702)386-5401

State of New Hampshire
Department of Education
Office of Teacher Education
and Professional Standards
State Office Park South
101 Pleasant Street
Concord, New Hampshire
03301
(603)271-2407

State of New Jersey
Department of Education
Office of Teacher Certification
and Academic Credentials
3535 Quakerbridge Road
CN 503
Trenton, New Jersey 08625-
0503
(609)984-1216

State of New Mexico
Department of Education
Teacher Education and
Certification Division
Education Building
300 Don Gaspar
Santa Fe, New Mexico 87501-
2786
(505)827-6635

State of New York
Department of Education
Division of Teacher
    Certification
Cultural Education Center
Albany, New York 12230
(518)474-3901

State of North Carolina
Department of Public
    Instruction
Division of Certification
116 West Edenton Street
Education Building
Raleigh, North Carolina
    27603-1712
(919)733-4125

Addresses of State Teacher Certification Offices

State of North Dakota
Department of Public
    Instruction
Office of Teacher Certification
Bismarck, North Dakota   58505
(701)224-2264

State of Ohio
Department of Education
Division of Teacher
Education and Certification
Ohio Departments Building
Room 1012
65 South Front Street
Columbus, Ohio   43215
(614)466-3593

State of Oklahoma
Department of Education
Section of Teacher
    Certification
Oliver Hodge
    Memorial Building
Room 232
2500 North Lincoln Boulevard
Oklahoma City, Oklahoma
    73105-4599
(405)521-3337

State of Oregon
Department of Education
Teacher Standards and
    Practices Commission
630 Center Street NE, Suite
200
Salem, Oregon   97310-0320
(503)378-3586

State of Pennsylvania
Department of Education
Bureau of Teacher Preparation
and Certification
Division of Teacher Education
333 Market Street
Harrisburg, Pennsylvania
    17126-0333
(717)787-2967

State of Rhode Island and
    Providence Plantations
Department of Education
Roger Williams Building
22 Hayes Street
Providence, Rhode Island
02908
(401)277-2675

State of South Carolina
Department of Education
Teacher Education
    and Certification
1015 Rutledge Building
1429 Senate Street
Columbia, South Carolina
29201
(803)734-8466

State of South Dakota
Division of Elementary
and Secondary Education
Teacher Certification Office
Kneip Office Building
700 North Illinois Street
Pierre, South Dakota   57501-
2293
(605)773-3553

State of Tennessee
Department of Education
Office of Teacher Education
and Certification
Cordell Hull Building
Room 125
Nashville, Tennessee   37219-
5338
(615)320-3163

State of Texas
Texas Education Agency
Division of Teacher
    Certification
1701 North Congress Avenue
Austin, Texas   78701-1494
(512)463-8976

Addresses of State Teacher Certification Offices

State of Utah
Board of Education
Division of Curriculum
  and Instruction
Teacher Certification
250 East 500 South
Salt Lake City, Utah 84111
(801)533-5965

State of Vermont
Department of Education
Teacher Certification
State Office Building
Montpelier, Vermont 05602
(802)828-2445

Commonwealth of Virginia
Department of Education
Division of Teacher
Education and Certification
P.O. Box 6 Q
Richmond, Virginia 23216-2060
(804)225-2097

State of Washington
Superintendent of
  Public Instruction
Professional Certification
Office
Old Capitol Building
Mail Stop FG-11
Olympia, Washington 98504
(206)753-2751

State of West Virginia
Department of Education
Director of Educational
Personnel Certification
1900 Washington Street, E.
Charleston, West Virginia
  25305
(304)348-7010

State of Wisconsin
Department of Public
  Instruction
Certification Section
125 South Webster Street
P.O. Box 7841
Madison, Wisconsin 53707
(608)266-1027

State of Wyoming
Department of Education
Certification/Licensing Unit
Hathaway Building
Cheyenne, Wyoming 82002
(307)777-6261

District of Columbia
Director,
Department of Certification
and Accreditation
415 12th Street, NW
Room 1004
Washington, D.C. 20004
(202)724-4230

Alternative Routes to the Classroom

Many states have recognized the critical shortages of teachers by passing special legislation to attract personnel from other fields into education. These college graduates have not completed the traditional education courses nor met state certification standards. In return for a beginning assignment in the classroom, they agree to attend after-school education workshops in conjunction with an intensive on-the-job training program. Such plans may go a great distance in addressing the national criticism of the declining ability of new teachers -- and provide a reliable pool of competent educators.

School districts design their own programs (within state guidelines) to train these "nontraditional" teachers, who are, for a predetermined period, granted "emergency" or "provisional" certification until regular or permanent state certification is obtained. What can you expect from the various programs? They have a number of elements in common. For instance, a bachelor's degree from an accredited four-year college is a prerequisite. Each participant agrees to attend after-school classes, workshops, and seminars on current educational theory and practice. And supervising teachers or mentors closely evaluate the performance of each trainee.

Of course, each district will require successful completion of a minimum skills proficiency examination on the part of the new teacher.

The point is a simple one -- if your state offers "nontraditional" teaching applicants the chance to become teachers, and if you are willing to meet the requirements set forth by the local district, you can transform your previous training into a new career in teaching.

What area of teaching should you enter? Consider your background and think of the applications your experience might have to young people. Accountants, computer analysts, data processors, and office managers might make excellent teachers of business education or computer-related courses. Athletes often are instructors of physical education, or coaches of school teams. Electricians, plumbers, carpenters, and mechanics have experience that is well-suited to vocational classes. Engineers and nurses may provide backgrounds in science, biology, drafting, physics, or chemistry. Many musicians, artists, or actors make top-notch fine arts instructors. And secretaries and administrative assistants possess valuable skills that can be passed on in typing and shorthand classes.

Consult your State Department of Education and the local school district where you wish to teach to determine if they offer an alternative route to the classroom.

Local School District Application

Hiring in education is done strictly at the local level. While states enforce teacher certification requirements, it's the responsibility of local boards of education to determine the number of professional staff they wish to employ. As a prospective teacher you must complete a battery of forms and documents for each local school district to which you apply. This is standard (albeit tiresome) procedure.

A local district employment application requires much more information than the application you will have completed to receive your state certificate. Typically, you will be asked to provide the following:

- Position desired
- Personal and academic background information
- Student teaching experience
- Teaching experience
- Substitute teaching experience
- State certification
- Experience other than teaching
- References
- Extracurricular training information

You should also be prepared to respond to essay questions, inquiries to your moral character and related matters. In addition, you should be ready to sign an affidavit testifying to the truthfulness of your responses.

Carefully consider an appropriate, well-worded reply to each essay question. Local school boards use these preliminary questions to go behind the purely superficial facts of your application and evaluate your individual philosophy of teaching. Proper grammar and correct punctuation should be reflected in your answers. Don't overlook legibility either, since the essays are frequently required to be hand-written rather than typed. A teacher is expected to exhibit a neat penmanship for the variety of writing done in school -- chalkboard, overhead transparencies, lesson plans, etc. Compose a rough draft of your answers before transferring them to the application form.

Three of the most common questions you're likely to encounter on an application from a local school district are:

Give the reasons for your choice of teaching as a profession.

Why do you want to teach in our district's public schools?

What do you hope to accomplish as a teacher?

Before completing your application, work out detailed, coherent responses to these questions so that your answers will come easily as you write them.

Finally, the entire credentials file from your college or university must be submitted for review by local school board authorities. Included in the file maintained in the placement office are your official college transcripts, record of student teaching and personal references.

Applications usually remain active for a period of one year from the date they are first received by the Board of Education. If you have not been called in for an interview during that time, it is your responsibility to notify (in writing) the local school district that you want them to keep your application under consideration. In that notification letter you should update information about your activities (employment, further training, etc.) since your original application was filed.

More Forms

Extensive supporting documentation must accompany your application for employment. You cannot be considered for a teaching position without submitting evidence of: a current health examination; a police record check; a residency statement (mandated by law in many school districts); and proof of United States citizenship.

You must also take a loyalty oath. Affirmative action surveys and teacher rating evaluations (completed by at least three of your personal/professional acquaintances) are also required.

There exists much unavoidable overlapping in the types of information requested by your State Board of Education (for issuance of a teaching certificate) and that requested by each local school district. Taking into account that you may be applying to several school districts, the paperwork will very likely become time-consuming and expensive. Regard this initial stage of your search for a classroom as the "trial by form." You will telephone many people, schedule appointments, visit different locations and correspond with a variety of administrative agencies in putting together your application.

Here are a few useful tips that will ease you through the maze of forms without a stumble:

Maintain a daily log of your activities. Note the results of each activity.

When seeking information, write the names of individuals you are contacting in your log. Address your correspondence to these individuals.

Keep copies of each letter, request and document you send. Mail does get lost or misdirected.

Provide a separate and secure location for all your material connected with the application process.

Telephone your references to be certain they have received the forms needed for your evaluation. (Beware: one missing document will stop the entire application process).

Doublecheck your application and all supporting papers for accuracy, grammar, spelling and completeness.

Chart of Required Teaching Forms

Name of Form	Required by State	Required by Local District
Application for state certificate	X	
Application for employment		X
Health examination		X
Teacher rating/ reference evaluation		X
Moral character questions	X	X
Police record check		X
Affirmative action survey		X
College transcripts	X	X
Student teaching record	X	X
Residency statement		X
Proof of U.S. citizenship	X	X
Loyalty oath		X

Sample Forms

On the following pages, you will find facsimiles of some of the most important forms you are likely to face as an applicant for a teaching position. These include: an application for state certification; an application for certificated employment; an affirmative action survey; a reference form; and a loyalty oath.

Remember that differences in actual wording and setup are to be expected in filling out the actual forms necessary to apply for a certificate or a position; use these examples as an overview of common questions and presentations.

APPLICATION FOR
STATE CERTIFICATION

* PLEASE TYPE OR PRINT * Carefully complete all appropriate sections
If additional space is needed at any point, please attach separate sheet.

PERSONAL DATA	Social Security Number:	Birth Date: (Mo/Dy/Yr)	Telephone:

Place of Birth (City and State)	U.S. Citizen? ☐ Yes ☐ No	If not, of what country?

Ms. ☐ Mrs. ☐ Miss ☐ Mr. ☐	Last	First	Middle	Maiden or Suffix

Present Mailing Address:	Street or Route No.	City	County	State	Zip

Permanent Address:	Street or Route No.	City	County	State	Zip

ACADEMIC RECORD	Location (City, State)	Yrs. Attended (From/To)	Date of Grad.	Kind of Degree	Sem. Hrs. Credit	Major
High School						
Colleges: 1.						
2.						
3.						
4.						

(Please list the exact name under which you were registered at the above institutions.)

FULL-TIME TEACHING EXPERIENCE

School Year	State	District (County)	School	Grades taught, or if departmentalized, subjects taught	No. months taught in school term	Type Certificate held
19 - 19						
19 - 19						
19 - 19						
19 - 19						
19 - 19						

I hereby apply for the following certificates:

Elementary ☐   Secondary ☐   Major(s)_____ Minor(s)_____

Special ☐   Type_____ (i.e. Special Education, Administration or Counseling, etc.)

Vocational Professional ☐   Special (Standard) ☐   Adult (Limited) ☐

(Identify Vocational Career Group or Vocational Subject to be taught:_____)

Substitute Elementary ☐   Substitute Secondary ☐

TRAINING INSTITUTION

For a new certificate, this part must be completed by a certification officer where applicant completed approved training program. Application must be accompanied by a complete set of official transcripts documenting the recommendation. The applicant has met the general education, professional education, and certification requirements of the approved program of teacher preparation in the following areas:

This program is approved by: STATE ☐   NCATE ☐

Degree and Major	Date Conferred	Institution
Date	Signature of Authorized Officer	

CHARACTER QUESTIONS: You must answer each question by writing in "Yes" or "No," whichever is true.

Have you ever been released or asked to resign from any educational position or school related employment because of misconduct or unsatisfactory service? _____

Have you ever resigned from an educational position while under investigation for misconduct or unsatisfactory service? _____

Have you ever failed to complete a contract for professional service in any educational position? _____

Have you ever held an educational position under a contract which was not renewed for the following year? _____

Have you ever had a certificate revoked or suspended? _____

Have you ever been denied a certificate for which you applied? _____

Have you ever surrendered a certificate before its expiration? _____

Have you ever been disciplined by a state agency responsible for certification of educators? _____

Have you ever been convicted of a felony, misdemeanor or major traffic violation (driving under the influence of intoxicants; reckless driving; fleeing or attempting to elude a police officer; driving while license is suspended or revoked or beyond license restrictions; or failure to perform the duties of a driver or witness at an accident)? If you answer "yes," a certified true copy of the court record must accompany this application. _____

Have you ever been arrested for any offense (other than a minor traffic violation) which is still pending in the courts? _____

Have you ever pled Nolo Contendere relative to any charge of misdemeanor, felony or major traffic violation? _____

Any "yes" answer must be explained fully, using a separate sheet.

NOTARIZATION (Must be completed by all applicants)

Sworn and subscribed before me this _____ *day of* _____ *, 19____.*

My commission expires _____

_____
Signature of Notary

(If a notary public is not available, a Postmaster may witness this affidavit.)

I certify that the statements made by me in this application are true and correct to the best of my knowledge. This becomes a part of my official record.

_____
Signature of Applicant

APPLICATION FOR CERTIFICATED EMPLOYMENT

PERSONAL INFORMATION

Date_____

Name (Last/First/Middle/Maiden)_____

Address_____ Telephone_____

Date of Birth_____ Birthplace_____

Social Security Number_____

Marital Status_____ Sex_____ Citizen of U.S.?_____

ACADEMIC INFORMATION

	NAME AND ADDRESS	PROGRAM OR COURSE	DEGREE AND MAJOR	YEAR OF GRAD	DATES ATTENDED	SEMESTER HOURS
HIGH SCHOOL						
COLLEGE OR UNIVERSITY (UNDERGRAD.)						
GRADUATE SCHOOL						
ADDITIONAL COURSES AND WORKSHOPS						

STUDENT TEACHING EXPERIENCE

School System	Subject and Grade	No. of Wks.	Supervisor	Address

TEACHING EXPERIENCE

School System	Position Held	From MO/YR	To MO/YR	Name of Superintendent	Address of Superintendent

SUBSTITUTE TEACHING EXPERIENCE

School Districts/ Program Mailing Address	Grades and/or Secondary Subjects Taught	From MO/YR	To MO/YR

CERTIFICATION INFORMATION

What type of certificate do you possess?

What is its date of issue?

What is its date of expiration?

By what state was it issued?

EXPERIENCE OTHER THAN TEACHING
(Include military service)

From MO/YR	To MO/YR	Firm or employer	Position (specify if full-time)	Reason for leaving

REFERENCES
(Principals, supervisors, or others with firsthand knowledge of your professional performance.)

Name	Address	Official position

POSITION DESIRED

ELEMENTARY TEACHERS: List grade preferred.

(first choice):_____

(second choice):_____

Are you prepared to teach: Art___   Music___   P.E.___

Would you be agreeable to teaching in a rural school?___

SECONDARY TEACHERS: List grades you are qualified to teach.

(first choice):_____

(second choice):_____

(third choice):_____

List subjects you are qualified to teach.

(first choice):_____

(second choice):_____

(third choice):_____

Please place a check mark to the left of student activities you can manage.

__Chorus   __School Paper   __Dramatics   __Golf   __Tennis

__Band   __School clubs   __Basketball   __Gymnastics   __Track

__Orchestra   __Forensics   __Football   __Swimming   __Volleyball

MORAL CHARACTER DETERMINATION

Please answer "yes" or "no" to the left of each question.

_____   Have you ever resigned from a position rather than face disciplinary action?

_____   Has any disciplinary action been brought against you which resulted in your being discharged from employment?

_____   Did you ever receive a discharge from the Armed Forces of the United States which was other than "honorable" or which was issued under other than honorable circumstances?

_____   Have you ever been convicted of any crime (felony or misdemeanor)?

_____   Are you now under charges for any crime (felony or misdemeanor)?

_____   Have you ever forfeited bail bond posted to guarantee your appearance in court to answer any charges?

_____   Have you ever had a teaching credential revoked, suspended, or annulled?

If you've answered "yes" to any of the above questions, you must attach a separate statement providing full pertinent details.

YOU WILL BE REQUIRED TO PROVIDE A POLICE CHECK BEFORE BEING HIRED. IF YOU HAVE A CONVICTION RECORD, YOUR EMPLOYMENT WILL DEPEND ON THE NUMBER, NATURE, AND RECENTNESS OF THE OFFENSES.

OTHER

How did you hear about this position?

    ___ Newspaper

    ___ School Employee

    ___ School Publication

    ___ Other (explain below)

Compose a brief (one page <u>handwritten</u>) essay in response to each of the following.

Give the reasons for your choice of teaching as a profession.

Why do you want to teach in our district's public schools?

What do you expect to accomplish as a teacher?

AFFIDAVIT

Under the penalties of perjury, I declare and affirm that the statements made in the foregoing application, including accompanying statements and transcriptions, are true and correct.

Date
_____

Signature of Applicant
_____

VOLUNTARY AFFIRMATIVE ACTION SURVEY

The information we ask you to provide below will not affect your employment or be available, or used in, any selection process. It will be used by the Personnel Department to compile statistics to support our Affirmative Action objectives. This information will be kept confidential.

Position applying for:_____

Date of application:_____

Sex: _____ Female _____ Male

Racial/Ethnic Data:

_____ **White:** A person having origins in any of the peoples of Europe, North Africa, or the Middle East who is not of Hispanic origin.

_____ **Black:** A person having origins in any of the black racial groups of Africa who is not of Hispanic origin.

_____ **Hispanic:** A person of Mexican, Puerto Rican, Cuban, South American, or other Spanish culture or origin, regardless of race.

_____ **Asian or Pacific Islander:** A person having origins in any of the original peoples of the Far East, Southeast Asia, the Indian subcontinent, or the Pacific Islands. This area includes, for example, China, India, Japan, Korea, the Phillipines, and Somoa.

_____ **American Indian or Alaskan Native:** A person having origins in any of the original peoples of North America, and who maintains cultural identification through tribal affiliation or community recognition.

HANDICAPPED STATUS:

Definitions for disabling or handicapping conditions: Any person who:

has a physical or mental impairment which substantially limits one or more of such person's major life activities; or,

has a record of such impairment; or,

is regarded as having such an impairment.

Do any of these conditions apply to you? _____ Yes _____ No

Date of birth (Month/Day/Year) _____

Signature_____

Date: _____

CONFIDENTIAL
TEACHER REFERENCE

TO: _____
Name of Reference (Please Print)

Applicant's name _____

Official Title _____

Date _____

Please Check the Appropriate Column	Poor	Below Avg.	Avg.	Above Avg.	Exc.
Personality -- shows those qualities that make teaching forceful and effective, such as: a pleasant, cheerful disposition, enthusiasm, and an appealing manner with pupils and others.					
Personal Appearance -- shows the type of grooming which reflects neatness, attentiveness, and appropriateness of attire.					
Physical Health -- has posture and bearing which gives evidence of energy and vitality in daily responsibilities.					
Emotional Stability -- has control of emotions which results in a general moderateness.					
Initiative -- has the quality of seeing what needs to be done and is judicious in doing it with or without direction.					
Ability to Work With Others -- has a cooperative and open-minded attitude in working with others in the solution of mutual problems. Respects the opinions, abilities, and contributions of others.					
Reliability -- is consistent, dependable, and accurate in carrying responsibilities to a successful conclusion.					
Ability to Stimulate Learning -- maintains a classroom situation which stimulates the maximum growth of individual pupils.					
Sympathetic Understanding of Children -- shows a sincere interest in children and in the solution of their problems.					
Ability to Control -- employs teaching procedures that reveal poise, inspire confidence of pupils, and command their respect.					
Professional Growth -- Is willing to examine his teaching effectiveness and constantly seeks better procedures.					
Community Relationships -- has ability to meet community-school situations with poise, understanding, and tact, resulting in friendly relationships.					
Professional Attitudes -- participates in activities which improve the status of the profession as a whole and of individual teachers.					

This information will be treated confidentially.   Signed _____

TEACHER OATH

STATE OF:_____

COUNTY OF:_____

    I do solemnly swear (or affirm) that I will support the Constitution of the United States of America and the constitution of the state of   , and that I will faithfully discharge the duties of teacher according to the best of my ability.

_____

         Signature

_____

         Notary

In and for

_____

County

My commission expires _____, 19___

CHAPTER SUMMARY

State certification is a prerequisite that must be obtained before local school districts can consider your employment.

Your present occupation can be converted into a new teaching career if your state or school district has an alternative route to the classroom program.

Apply for your state certificate (or license) immediately after graduation.

Type or print when entering information on official documents. Fill out all forms completely.

Set a professional goal of attaining state certification in more than one teaching field.

Keep informed of changes in your state's certification requirements; renew your certificate before its expiration date.

Hiring in education is done entirely at the local level.

Local school districts require a detailed application and numerous supporting documents before they will process your application.

Pay close attention to essay questions on your application.

Information requested by your state certification office will overlap with information requested by the local school district.

Consider the task of completing the many forms and documents to be a job in itself, but one that will help you achieve your career goal of teaching.

Two: Professional Examinations -- Testing The Teachers

Teachers and Tests: The State Level

Teacher testing examinations constitute a large component of the state certification process as well as local school district hiring decisions. Recently enacted educational reform legislation has called for even greater testing of teachers and the adherence to more stringent academic standards. Before you receive that first classroom assignment, rest assured that you will have become an expert in taking (and passing) tests.

States use different names for their testing programs: Teacher Proficiency Testing, Basic Skills Competency Testing, Pre-Professional Skills Test, Teacher Certification Testing Program or Basic Educational Skills Test. Regardless of their names, the tests are designed to place the most competent applicants in our public schools.

There are several common elements among the various state teacher testing programs:

> The tests are required by law before an initial teaching certificate can be issued.

> The NTE (National Teacher Examinations) Core Battery Tests and Specialty Area Tests may be used for State Certification.

> Teacher tests are in addition to all other course requirements for issuance of a certificate.

> Subject areas to be tested include: English, reading, writing, spelling, mathematics and professional knowledge.

> Applicants who fail any or all of the testing program may be retested after a waiting period. Remedial help is offered to these applicants.

> State competency testing programs are done in

conjunction with initial teacher certification - they do not replace any part of a local school district's own testing program.

Experienced teachers may also be required to participate in a teacher testing program for renewal of their certificates.

Teacher testing is a permanent feature of the state certification process.

Each state determines its own standards for passing.

Fees are required.

Constitution Tests

You must show evidence of proficiency in the United States Constitution and the constitution of the state where you are seeking a teaching position.

This is a standard requirement for initial state certification. Generally, these two test requirements are met when you complete an approved teacher training program. In certain special circumstances (for example, a teacher seeking a provisional certificate without completing an education program) you may not have fulfilled this prerequisite. Consult with your State Board of Education's Certification Division for advice in these unusual cases.

Teachers and Tests: The Local Level

States establish their own minimum standards for teacher certification. Once the state issues you a teaching certificate, the local school district is free to impose additional requirements for employment, so long as the basic state guidelines are met. These local requirements may include the district's own competency testing program (English, math, spelling, etc.) as well as practical examinations in certain teaching areas. For example, a vocational teacher may be asked to demonstrate specific wood-working techniques while a physical education teacher may be required to pass a life-saving test.

Your local school district will have the complete details of their current teacher testing program for employment. Get answers to these questions:

- *What competency tests are required?*

- *Where will the tests be given?*

- *When are the tests offered?*

- *What are passing scores?*

- *Is remedial assistance available?*

- *How much do the tests cost?*

Introduction to the NTE

The National Teacher Examination, or NTE, is a nationwide, objective test of academic achievement for college graduates majoring in education. It is administered by the Educational Testing Service of Princeton, New Jersey. Although the NTE is a widely recognized testing program for teachers, each state is free to develop its own competency testing plan. Standards for passing the NTE (or any teacher examination) are also decided at the state level.

A new graduate may ignore or decide against taking the NTE. After all, if the state in which he or she is seeking a position does not require the test, why bother? That type of thinking, however, is a mistake. Whether or not it's state required for issuance of a teaching certificate, give high priority to passing the NTE.

Why? State programs are by their nature limited in scope. They do not provide an overall perspective or feedback on how you compare academically to other teachers. NTE results have the advantage of ranking your score with tens of thousands of teaching candidates across the United States.

In your career as an educator, the successful completion of the NTE is regarded as a mark of excellence, professionalism and distinction. It is comparable to the Bar examination for lawyers or the CPA examination for accountants. Register for the NTE -- now!

Organization of the NTE

The NTE is divided into two distinct sections: Core Battery Tests and Specialty Area Tests. Usually, a new graduate in education will register for all three Core Battery Tests and one Specialty Area Test. The first section is designed to test the standard information content of your college teaching program, while the other section assesses comprehension in your major field of study.

What format do the tests take? Their structure is similar to that of other professional examinations. A 30-minute essay on an assigned topic is required for the Writing component of the Test of Communication Skills; all the other Core Battery and Specialty Area tests are multiple-choice.

It's easier to view the structure of the NTE using an outline form:

I. *Core Battery Tests*

A. Test of Communication Skills

    1. Listening
    2. Reading
    3. Writing

B. Test of General Knowledge

    1. Literature and Fine Arts
    2. Mathematics
    3. Science
    4. Social Studies

C. Test of Professional Knowledge

II. Specialty Area Tests (based on college majors)

Art Education
Audiology
Biology and General Science
Business Education
Chemistry, Physics and General Science
Early Childhood Education (ages 3-8)
Education in the Elementary School (grades 1-8)
Education of Mentally Retarded Students
Educational Administration and Supervision
English Language and Literature
French
German
Home Economics Education
Industrial Arts Education
Introduction to the Teaching of Reading
Library Media Specialist
Mathematics
Music Education
Physical Education
Reading Specialist
School Guidance and Counseling
Social Studies
Spanish
Special Education
Speech Communication
Speech-Language Pathology

NOTE: There is an NTE Specialty Area Test in Agriculture offered in Louisiana, South Carolina and California.

Sample Test Schedule and Fees

Each Core Battery and Specialty Area Test lasts for two hours. If you register for all three Core Battery Tests and one Specialty Area Test, your testing schedule will look something like this:

Core Battery Tests

8:00 - 8:30 a.m.	Registration/Orientation
8:30 - 10:30 a.m.	Test of Communication Skills
11:15 a.m. - 1:15 p.m.	Test of General Knowledge
1:15 - 2:30 p.m.	Lunch
2:30 - 4:30 p.m.	Test of Professional Knowledge
4:40 p.m.	Dismissal

Specialty Area Tests

8:30 - 9:00 a.m.	Registration/Orientation
9:00 - 11:00 a.m.	Specialty Area Tests
11:15 a.m.	Dismissal

The NTE is always administered on Saturdays. Core Battery and Specialty Area Tests are scheduled two or three weeks apart with the entire NTE program being offered three times during an academic year.

Current fees (subject to change) for the NTE are:

One Core Battery Test	$28.00
Two Core Battery Tests (same date)	$38.00
Three Core Battery Tests (same date)	$48.00
Specialty Area Test	$35.00

Expect to pay a minimum of $83.00 if you register for all three Core Battery Tests along with your Specialty Area Test.

Additional fees are required for change of registration, late registration, score verification and other special circumstances.

Test Preparation

"How do I prepare for the NTE?" Relax! You've already completed your preparation for the NTE. Just review your accomplishments so far -- they're quite impressive. You have:

Successfully finished four-year undergraduate program of teacher training.

Taught one year as student-teacher.

Attended numerous seminars, lectures, and workshops.

Participated in group discussions and class projects.

Read innumerable books, articles, and reports.

Taken daily notes in each class.

Written detailed research papers.

Passed quarterly, midterm and final examinations in both essay and multiple choice formats.

The NTE is a means for synthesizing information you're well-acquainted with; it's one culminating mark of achievement in the teaching profession -- and whether you realize it or not, you're ready.

In case you can't relax or just need a few helpful tips to attain that passing score, here's some sound advice that should put you over the top:

Take the NTE as early as possible. Recent college graduates generally score best.

Enroll in an established NTE review program. Consult with your college placement office for recommendations.

Purchase one of the many commercially available NTE study guides from your local bookstore. They're inexpensive ($10.00 - $15.00) and often contain excellent practice tests that you can drill from using realistic time limitations.

Familiarize yourself with the current NTE Bulletin of Information well in advance of the Saturday test date.

Be prompt on test day; give yourself extra travel time to the test site.

Check that you have all the supplies and material mentioned in the Bulletin: photo identification; admission ticket; completed Critical Information Form; and No. 2 pencils (sharpened).

Follow all instructions in your test booklet -- exactly.

As you take the test, bear in mind that you will perform best when you approach each question in a relaxed, confident manner.

Pace yourself. Don't spend an inordinate amount of time on questions you find difficult. All questions have equal value within each separately timed section. As you take the examination, remember that there will be several unfamiliar questions. This is normal testing design. You can still receive a high passing score without knowing all the answers.

Guess -- sometimes. You should definitely guess (rather than leave blank) answers on the Core Battery Tests: Communication Skills, General Knowledge, and Professional Knowledge. There is no penalty for guessing here, since your score is based on the total number of correct responses. On the other hand, there *is* a penalty for incorrect answers in the Specialty Area Tests. A fraction of a point for each incorrect answer is subtracted from your total correct responses. Guess in this section only if you have some knowledge of the question and can eliminate one or more of the choices; otherwise, leave the question blank.

Passing the NTE Depends on...

Passing the NTE depends to some extent on the state where you live.   States that mandate the NTE for certification determine their own minimum scores.   These scores can and do change every few years.   Consult with your State Department of Education to find their exact standards for the NTE.   Minimum passing scores have been rising and should continue to do so as the public demands increased professional standards for teachers.

Here is a brief chart that illustrates the differences among six states regarding required NTE scores on the Core Battery Tests.*

	Communication Skills	General Knowledge	Professional Knowledge
Hawaii	647	648	651
Louisiana	645	644	645
Mississippi	647	642	645
New Mexico	644	645	630
New York	650	649	646
Tennessee	640	637	631

*Source: State Departments of Education

For More Information About the NTE

The NTE is administered by the Educational Testing Service (ETS) of Princeton, New Jersey. They maintain a hotline and can help you if you have questions about registration or test administration. Call (609)771-7670 Monday through Friday, between 8:30 a.m. and 9:00 p.m. Eastern time.

You can obtain the current NTE Bulletin of Information from your college placement office or by writing to:

> NTE Programs
> Educational Testing Service
> CN 6050
> Princeton, New Jersey 08541-6050

The Bulletin will contain the complete listing of test sites, dates and registration materials for the next NTE.

Don't Underestimate the NTE

Once you have achieved your initial test scores for certification and have begun teaching, you may even want to go back and take a second Specialty Area examination. The job market for teachers is constantly changing; your interests may also change after you have entered the profession. Passing additional NTE Specialty Area Tests as part of your overall career goal of dual state certification is the best job insurance available. You will pay a premium in terms of time, money and effort spent studying, but reap benefits in terms of job security. You'll broaden your opportunities. And you will not be required to take the Core Battery Tests again when trying for a second certificate. An ideal combination of NTE Specialty Area Tests that maximizes your total job prospects might be one in which there is one test intended as the focus of your work in elementary school, and another that covers a high school subject in your area of interest.

Overview of Teacher Testing

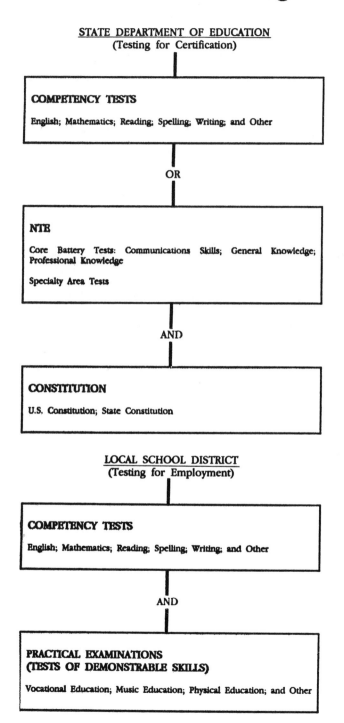

STATE DEPARTMENT OF EDUCATION
(Testing for Certification)

COMPETENCY TESTS

English; Mathematics; Reading; Spelling; Writing; and Other

OR

NTE

Core Battery Tests: Communications Skills; General Knowledge; Professional Knowledge

Specialty Area Tests

AND

CONSTITUTION

U.S. Constitution; State Constitution

LOCAL SCHOOL DISTRICT
(Testing for Employment)

COMPETENCY TESTS

English; Mathematics; Reading; Spelling; Writing; and Other

AND

**PRACTICAL EXAMINATIONS
(TESTS OF DEMONSTRABLE SKILLS)**

Vocational Education; Music Education; Physical Education; and Other

Hiring Trends in Education: How Do They Affect What Tests to Take?

Economic laws of supply and demand affect teaching jobs no less than jobs in other fields. If there is an oversupply of teachers within a particular subject area, those people expecting to teach that discipline will encounter a more difficult job search. Conversely, graduates with a state certificate in one or more subject areas where there is little competition will face a much easier job search.

Although trends can (and will!) change, this chart reflects current information from several states regarding their areas of teacher shortage as well as their areas of oversupply. Consider this chart as you select your Specialty Area Tests, and in planning your overall teaching career. Remember the important edge you can derive from dual state certification. Also, note that *where* you plan on teaching can have as great an impact on your chances for a succesful job hunt as *what* you plan on teaching.

AREAS OF TEACHER SHORTAGE:

Bilingual Education/ Computer Education/ Industrial Arts/ Library Science/ Mathematics/ Biology/ Chemistry/ General Science/ Physical Science/ Physics/ Special Education (Behavior Disordered; Emotionally Disturbed; Learning Disabled; Speech-Hearing Impaired; Physically Handicapped; Visually Impaired)

AREAS OF TEACHER OVERSUPPLY:

Art/ Home Economics/ Music/ Social Studies/ Physical Education

---

CHAPTER SUMMARY

Teachers are subject to a battery of competency tests as part of the state certification process.

Local school districts also utilize a variety of teacher tests, including practical examinations, to screen job applicants.

The NTE is the only standardized, nationwide test for teachers; it should be taken regardless of whether or not it is a state certification requirement.

Your successful completion of a four-year training program in education has prepared you for the NTE and all other teacher competency tests.

Each state determines the extent of its teacher testing program as well as mandating minimum passing scores for the NTE.

The changing job market for teachers necessitates taking more than one NTE Specialty Area Test - dual certification should be a career goal.

Three:
The Job Search

Remember Your Resume

A resume is a summary or brief account of your personal, educational and professional qualifications in applying for a job. Resumes are widely used in education. In your search for a teaching position, it is important to devote the time and effort necessary to compose a well-written, well-planned resume.

Look upon your resume as a multi-faceted document. It is an excellent means for responding to specific newspaper or college placement office job listings. Also, you can submit your resume to several school districts simultaneously as an initial method for inquiring into available teaching positions. Use your resume to focus attention on those aspects of your background that are neglected or glossed over by all the other preset forms. Remember, your resume is the only unique, personal statement that you will have the opportunity of "individualizing."

You may ask, "What topics or headings should I include in my resume?" "What questions should my resume answer?" Following is a suggested format with sample questions. Keep in mind that the resume is *your* document. Some sections may not be relevant to you; you may want to add other sections. Change the resume's format to best suit your needs and illustrate your commitment to teaching.

Make Sure Your Resume Includes:

Career Objective. What do you hope to accomplish as a teacher? (One or two sentences only).

Education. What college degree(s) have you been awarded? Are you currently enrolled in a graduate or continuing education program?

Student Teaching. Where did you student teach? Who were your supervising teacher and principal? What grade/subject did you teach?

School Related Activities. Have you ever coached a sports team? Did you participate in any school clubs or organizations?

Certification. What type of state teaching certificate do you possess? When did you receive it? When is its expiration date?

Work Experience. Have you been previously employed by another school system?

Professional Associations. Are you a member of any professional associations in education? Have you contributed articles to any professional journals?

69

Extras Count!

Extra-curricular activities that you participated in during college could give you an edge in getting that preliminary interview. Every remotely relevant club, sport, or organization of which you were a member should probably appear in your resume. Local districts look for teachers who can fulfill many functions in a school building. The English teacher who has the experience to direct students in after-school plays, or the math teacher who knows how to coach children's sports is regarded as a more valuable applicant than one who lacks such extra skills.

Here is a partial list of school sports and extra-curricular activities to consider as you prepare your resume:

SCHOOL SPORTS:

Baseball	Golf	Track
Basketball	Gymnastics	Trainer
Cheerleading	Intramurals	Water Polo
Cross-Country	R.O.T.C.	Wrestling
Drill-Team	Swimming	Volleyball
Football	Tennis	Soccer

SCHOOL ACTIVITIES:

Debate	Newspaper
Drama	Student Government
Music-choral	Textbook Management
Music-instrumental	Yearbook

Resume Mechanics

Know your audience. Your resume will be read by personnel specialists of local school districts. They are busy people who review hundreds of forms daily. Show concern for their hectic schedules by remembering that your resume is more likely to be scanned than read. Be brief but compelling.

What unique talents or experiences do you offer? If you were a busy superintendent with only twenty or thirty minutes to go through a pile of resumes, what would you be able to determine about an applicant's talents within the first sixty seconds? You will present yourself in a favorable light by following these basic guidelines for resume preparation:

Length: 1-2 pages. Keep it brief; one page is best for new college graduates.

Paper: 8 1/2" x 11" white or off-white. Any other color would be considered unprofessional. Use only a high quality paper.

Type: Pica or elite. Black ink only.

Margins: 1" - 1 1/2" on all four sides.

Grammar: Perfect English, spelling and punctuation. You're the teacher!

Appearance: Visually attractive. No marks, erasures, stains, etc.

Proofread: Mandatory. Have several people, including someone from the placement office, read your resume before you make copies.

Reproduction: No photocopies. Your resume should be typeset or word processed using a letter quality printer.

Sample Resume

MARGARET A. BAILEY
591 Lake Shore Plaza
Chicago, Illinois 60646
(312/123-0000)

CAREER OBJECTIVE

A classroom teaching position in the primary grades.
To foster the academic and social growth of
primary-age children.

EDUCATION

1987: B.A., Elementary Education,
      UNIVERSITY OF ILLINOIS, Champaign-Urbana

STUDENT TEACHING

1987: HAY PUBLIC SCHOOL, Smithville, Illinois
      Supervising Teacher -- Mrs. Evelyn Thomas
      Principal -- Mr. Edward Peterson
      Taught reading, spelling, and handwriting
      to 25 second-grade students.

SCHOOL ACTIVITIES

Literacy tutor volunteer, 1985-1987

Organized and acted in theatre workshop
project that performed children's classics
for disadvantaged city youngsters, 1986-1987.

Student Council secretary/treasurer, 1986-1987

CERTIFICATION

Illinois Elementary (K-9) Certificate

PROFESSIONAL ASSOCIATIONS

Association for Childhood Education
   International
National Association for the
   Education of Young Children

Sample Resume

STEPHEN R. ALEXANDER   (617)111-0001 (Home)
6224 Bay View Road   (617)100-1000 (Work)
Boston, Massachusetts 02127

CAREER OBJECTIVE

Develop a comprehensive high school mathematics program for gifted students.

EDUCATION

1985: M.S., Mathematics, UNIVERSITY OF MASSACHUSETTS, Amherst

1983: B.A., Elementary Education, NORTHEASTERN UNIVERSITY Boston

Additional graduate coursework in Secondary Education, Curriculum Studies, Gifted Education

CERTIFICATION

Massachusetts certificates in Math (Grades 9-12), Middle School (Grades 5-9)

WORK EXPERIENCE

Elementary mathematics resource coordinator, King Public School, Boston, Massachusetts, 1985 - present.

Eighth grade math teacher, Stevens Elementary, Quincy, Massachusetts, 1983-1985.

ACHIEVEMENTS

Wrote teacher's guide for computer-assisted instruction materials in mathematics, 1986

Inservice teacher facilitator on topic - "An Enriched Math Curriculum for Gifted Elementary Students," 1986

Organized gifted programs in math for elementary students, 1985-1986

Distinguished Teacher Award, 1985

Published workbook - *Problem Solving Techniques for the Accelerated Student*, Johnson Publications, Los Angeles, 1984

Member of Mathematics Curriculum Committee, State Board of Education, 1984

PROFESSIONAL ASSOCIATIONS

American Association for Gifted Children
American Mathematical Society
Educational Press Association of America
National Council of Teachers of Mathematics

Cover Letters

A resume is never sent in isolation. It should always be accompanied by a brief cover letter explaining your purpose in contacting the school district. While a resume is a general form that details your education, work history and achievements, a cover letter is specific. It is intended for one employer only. If you are submitting five resumes for consideration to five local districts, each resume would have its own separate and distinct cover letter. Your cover letter conveys evidence of your sincere interest in joining a school system's professional staff.

Conciseness is vital in cover letters -- approximately 200 words. (Again, personnel departments are busy places). Call the school district to request the name of the personnel manager. Direct your letter to that person's attention. It is usually a more efficient procedure to send mail to a person rather than a department. It also shows the people you want to reach that you are putting forth added effort in your job search.

In the opening paragraph, state the exact reason for mailing your resume.

Are you responding to a job advertisement initiated by the school board? If yes, give all the facts surrounding the ad -- where and when you saw the ad, name of position, job description, and so forth.

Are you inquiring into overall employment opportunities for your teaching area within that district? Highlight your background in the cover letter, and state one or two significant prior achievements that will show the reader what you can offer.

In the second paragraph, tell why you are interested in teaching for this school system. Refer to your enclosed resume and point out aspects of your education and background that support your employment.

Conclude the letter on a positive note that opens the door to further communication. Ask for a formal application for employment as well as any printed material the district publishes for potential employees. Provide your home telephone number and a stamped, self-addressed envelope for the district's convenience.

What format should you employ when writing your cover letter?

A cover letter is a business letter. Hiring decisions in education (as in most other areas) are based on logic. Simple facts, clearly expressed, will be helpful in getting a personal interview. Avoid any hint of familiarity or emotion in your writing. Just stick to the facts -- that's all!

Follow the same guidelines suggested for preparation of your resume when writing your cover letter, with one exception -- be sure that you never exceed one page in length. A cover letter using block form with every line beginning at the left margin is a currently popular style.

Possible Model for Cover Letter

Today's Date

Your Street Address
Your City, State, and Zip Code

Contact Person Name
Title
School or District
City, State, and Zip Code

Dear Mr. (Ms.) _____:

Specify the position you are seeking and outline your background. Give a concrete example of a viewpoint, accomplishment, or past experience that you can claim -- one that is of immediate interest to someone in charge of hiring teachers.

Elaborate upon your background, and display your knowledge of the district. If there are volunteer activities that are relevant to your search for a teaching position, detail them here.

Close the letter with a request for an interview and/or a formal application for employment. Enclose your daytime telephone number -- but be prepared to follow up with a telephone call of your own.

Sincerely yours,

(Signature)

Your full name (typed)

Sample Cover Letter

August 11, 1987

591 Lake Shore Plaza
Chicago, Illinois   60646

Paulette C. Williams
Manager of Human Resources
Illinois School District 15
Smithville, Illinois   61801

Dear Ms. Williams:

My enclosed resume is in response to last week's
advertisement for second-grade teachers that appeared in the
Daily Herald. As a recently graduated senior majoring in
Elementary Education, I realize the importance that
children's primary academic instruction plays in their total
growth and development.

During my four years of teacher training I've witnessed new
and exciting educational programs being implemented in
District 15. Besides fulfilling my practice teaching
experience in Smithville, I participated in District 15's
cooperative literacy tutoring program. Additionally, I
helped stage theatre workshop performances for many students
in local area public schools.

District 15 represents such high educational standards that
I welcome this opportunity to be considered for a faculty
position. Please send me a formal application for
employment and other pertinent information; you can contact
me at (312) 123-0000 to schedule a personal interview.

I look forward to meeting with you.

Sincerely,

Margaret A. Bailey
Margaret A. Bailey

Sample Cover Letter

June 14, 1987

6224 Bay View Road
Boston, Massachusetts
02127

George W. Michaels
Personnel Director
Pershing School District 10
Pershing, Massachusetts 02720

Dear Mr. Michaels:

The position of high school mathematics coordinator, as described in the June 8, 1987 edition of the Times, appears to provide just the type of challenging instructional leadership role I am seeking. I was especially intrigued by the statement "...must possess unique combination of interest in gifted math instruction along with demonstrated capability to write curriculum materials..." My thorough examination of your job advertisement convinced me to write and apply for the position.

In addition to completing extensive graduate studies in educating the gifted child, I helped implement accelerated math programs at both King Public School and Stevens Elementary. Having served on the State Board of Education's Mathematics Curriculum Committee, I hold a deep interest in improving the quality of curriculum materials. Although my background to-date has been at the elementary level, I have been studying secondary education and recently obtained a Massachusetts math certificate (grades 9-12) enabling me to teach at the high school level.

The enclosed resume further details my academic training, work experience, and educational achievements. It reflects concern, dedication, and enthusiasm for our profession of teaching; it's a record, I believe, that illustrates the qualities you are searching for in a high school mathematics coordinator.

Since summer vacation is already upon us, you can only contact me at my listed home number (617) 111-0001. Please call at your convenience so that we can arrange a personal interview to discuss the open position. I look forward to our meeting.

Sincerely,

Steven R. Alexander

Steven R. Alexander

Your Teaching Job Search Network

Many people are frightened when they encounter the term "networking." It often appears to apply to a high-level world of business, finance and government officials who, unlike someone beginning a job search, are already "established."

Actually, you already have a vast network of resources (encompassing both people and institutions) to assist in your job search. Consider the following sources. Each can be employed in specific job search strategies that will put you in a classroom; some suggestions follow each category.

College Professors: Ask professors familiar with your work if they can recommend local school districts who are seeking teachers in your subject area. Many college instructors have excellent contacts.

Student Teaching: You probably met several important people from your student teaching practicum. These might include a supervising teacher, principal, assistant principal, college advisor, and others. Call upon each one; they're valuable sources of information regarding present job openings.

College Placement Office: Register early at your placement office to take full advantage of the multitude of programs they offer.

Teacher Job Fairs: Attend a teacher recruitment fair in your area; they're sponsored by local colleges or school districts. Talk to the representatives; out-of-state districts may also be visiting your area in their search for teachers.

Newspaper Ads: Always check your paper's want ads -- school districts do advertise there. It's a traditional but still valid method of job searching. (Bear in mind, however, that competition is likely to be stiff for these

these advertised openings. You may want to use want ads more as a source for hiring *patterns* at a given district.)

Professional Associations: Join a professional association in your field of expertise; subscribe and contribute to the association's journal or newsletter; attend the association's regional and national meetings. Jobs are a topic of conversation on every association's "unwritten" agenda.

Alumni Organization: Participate in the activities of your college's alumni association. You'll meet alumni who are teachers, principals, and other educational personnel. What's good for the college could also prove to be beneficial to your employment prospects.

Volunteer Work: Schools recruit volunteer workers for a variety of paraprofessional tasks. Call a school or district you're interested in to inquire if they need volunteers. Volunteer work is a foot in the schoolhouse door that shouldn't be overlooked.

Friends/Relatives: Everyone seems to have a teacher in their family or knows a friend who teaches. How about you?

Private Employment Agency: Many school districts list classroom vacancies with private employment firms. Check an agency's reputation first before proceeding; private companies do charge fees for their services. Be particularly cautious about hard-sell firms that boast a "hidden" network of job contacts. Often, such networks consist of commercial mailing lists used to "dump" your resume on many desks at a time. Find out specifically what you're paying for and what you can expect in return.

Put all of these strategies together and you have a solid network of people and places that will yield you career opportunities in education. These strategies are not only good for finding your initial teaching position but are also worthwhile methods of professional advancement in later years.

Overview of the Teacher Job Search Network

College Professors   Newspaper Ads

Student Teaching

College Placement Office   Job Fairs

YOUR TEACHING CAREER

Professional Associations   Volunteer Work

Alumni Organization

Employment Agency   Friends/Relatives

Sub For Success

How can your job search be profitable, fun, and exciting while still focused on the business of finding full-time employment? The answer, for many, lies in becoming a substitute teacher.

As you've probably guessed by now, finding a full-time position as a teacher can be a daunting experience, one that carries with it a fair measure of rejection. Qualified substitutes, however, are always in demand.

Working as a substitute is an excellent job search strategy that offers: a daily wage; steady assignments; flexibility to work as many days per week as you wish; valuable experience; an expanded network of teaching contacts; and the opportunity to discover vacancies before they're officially advertised. Many new graduates plan on doing substitute work as a part of their overall job search. In this manner, they can research the local district and its schools on a first hand basis. Furthermore, they can sub in several districts simultaneously, simplifying the task of comparing the various programs, policies, benefits and so forth.

Subs develop an extensive network of referrals and career contacts in a very short time. The nature of the work provides constant interaction with key school officials, such as principals and assistant principals. Frequently at the end of a school day, a substitute will produce a resume, hand it to the principal, and ask if there are any permanent vacancies on the horizon. (Such action is not considered unprofessional -- principals can and do recommend candidates to the district's personnel department.) Substitute teachers, unlike new college graduates in education, are more inclined to receive strong job recommendations since they've already been observed and evaluated in classroom situations.

If, after graduation, you haven't been offered an assignment by the start of the next school year, you should probably sub and continue to expand your sources for job leads. Keep in mind, however, this one vital rule -- never pass up a full-time teaching position to remain a substitute!

Many teachers refuse permanent job offers waiting for that "perfect situation." *Don't wait!* Ideal assignments are non-existent, even for experienced teachers. The job is what you bring to it, not what it brings to you. Holding out for a combination of an ideal grade assignment, the right school district, the proper students, the highest compensation package, and the best schedule will indeed put you on the path to a lifetime career -- of substitute work. Be realistic: sub to find your teaching career, but avoid making substitute work your teaching career. Take the full-time position over the job as a sub.

Get Out of the House!

How can you best *keep* from getting the teaching position you want? Simple. Procrastination. It's easy to turn a job hunt into a private vacation at your expense. Just look at the Monday schedule of Mr. Larry Lately:

8:30 a.m.	Wakes up.
9:00	Breakfast.
10:00	Reads newspaper (sports section first).
11:00	Discovers job ad that sounds promising.
11:30	Begins writing cover letter.
12:00	Lunch.
1:00 p.m.	Waits for mail to see if School District #34 has answered his letter requesting employment information.
2:00	Still waiting - mail is late.
3:00	Continues writing cover letter, hopes to have it ready later in the week.
4:00	Mail arrives - no response from School District #34, but several past due notices have come in.
5:15	Calls his college placement office to inquire about current openings; listens to tape recorded message saying - "Please call during regular business hours, 8:30 a.m.-5:00 p.m., Monday-Friday."
5:30	Dinner.
6:15 - bed	Careful evaluation of Gilligan's Island reruns, evening news, and celebrity pinochle tournament.

Contrast Mr. Lately's job hunting procedures with those of Ms. Tina Timely:

6:15 a.m.	Wakes up.
6:45	Breakfast.
7:15	Commutes to neighborhood school for work as substitute teacher.
8:15	Assigned to 8th grade science class.
9:00 - 3:00 p.m.	Teaches departmental science classes, meets principal and assistant principal, and inquires about future staff openings at the end of the day.
4:00	Arrives home, reads newspaper and professional journals noting data on several job openings and upcoming educational conferences in her area.
5:30	Dinner.
6:30	Plans for the remainder of the week, including three more days of sub work and a personal interview at the district office.
7:30 - 9:30	Attends graduate level course in education at local branch of state university system.

What's the big difference? Larry is *passive,* Tina is *active.* Larry is at the mercy of his environment (the school district, the placement office's hours, even his own mailman), while Tina uses her time efficiently to pursue valuable leads and cultivate professional contacts. Getting a job requires constant activity and movement. Follow these guidelines to assure success in your job hunt:

Maintain a regular schedule during normal business hours. Such a schedule might include substitute or school volunteer work; going on personal interviews, and participating in professional conferences, seminars, and meetings. *Don't wait for a job to find you.*

Dress in a businesslike manner for each activity you attend.

Complete job hunting paperwork (answering want ads, writing cover letters, sending resumes, reading this book) only during evenings and weekends. Use business hours for contacts and work experience.

Enroll in a graduate level education course; keep in contact with your college professors.

Inside The College Placement Office

Education job searches frequently begin in a college placement office. What resources do such offices provide? What is the best approach to take when using one? To answer these questions, the following interview was conducted with Maxine K. Jacks, a career counselor specializing in educational placement with the Career Development and Placement Office at Northeastern Illinois University in Chicago, Illinois. It gives an in-depth look at the operation of the placement office in fulfilling vital tasks in the education marketplace. Consult your own college placement office for specific details on the services it offers.

What is the role of the placement office in finding jobs in education?

Our mission is twofold. We serve candidates seeking positions in an educational setting. This means primarily teaching jobs but could include a variety of administrative jobs as well. Local school districts also contact a college placement office when they have specific openings on their staffs. We assist in bringing applicants and employers together.

When do education majors come in contact with the placement office?

Typically, the first time most education majors hear about the placement office is during their senior year of student teaching experience. We sponsor a seminar at which each senior is given a packet of credentials forms to complete and return. They are registered with the placement office only upon completion of the entire credentials packet. Besides explaining the forms and how credentials are used in obtaining teaching positions, we provide important information about state certification requirements.

Is it useful for students to visit the placement office earlier than their senior year?

Definitely. Students need not wait until their senior

year to get acquainted with the placement office. They're welcome anytime to review the resources and programs we offer.

Do you have to be a current student to use the placement office?

No. Alumni of the college are also welcome to visit and utilize our facilities.

What job search assistance and resources can your office provide?

We marshall numerous aids for the job seeker. We maintain and distribute listings of all school districts in our region, arrange campus recruitment days, and provide updated information on the job market for teachers. At the request of faculty supervising student teachers, staff members will give workshops on resume writing and interview preparation emphasizing the needs of education majors. A video presentation, *Interviewing for Teachers,* can also be viewed by individuals or groups.

Our career resource library includes directories of public and private schools (local, county, state, national, and overseas); manuals on certification requirements; our bi-weekly vacancy list as well as exchange lists from other colleges and universities giving information about available education positions; binders of current salary schedules from school districts, and annually updated files of school district informational materials. The majority of this material is from our local area but out-of-state materials are also available. These are essential resources for an effective job search.

What is a credentials file? How important is a student's credentials file?

A credentials file is an individual folder of documents that we maintain for each student in education. Included in this file are a personal data sheet and letters of reference from the student's university supervisor, cooperating teacher(s), and others who observed actual classroom performance. It is difficult to obtain any teaching position without fairly strong recommendations from these key individuals.

Each student should realize it is imperative that all

credential file forms be completed in a professional manner: typed, accurate, and thorough. Proofread everything! Credentials files may or may not include a transcript depending on the particular placement office.

Are credential files required?

No. Opening a file is usually not required but is always highly recommended. It may prove impossible to obtain letters about one's student teaching if the file is not started until a number of years after graduation.

Are there different types of credentials files?

Credentials files can be either open or confidential -- in other words, not available to candidates. There are advantages to both types. Candidates with open files are able to read and have copies of the letters in their file and decide whether or not to include the letter. Confidential letters can be more candid in their comments and are sometimes preferred by school administrators.

Today, a large majority of files are open. Candidates can select those who will write letters to be included in their file. This list can and should change as the file is updated to reflect additional experience and education.

How often should teaching applicants update their credentials files?

Yearly updating is recommended because principals and superintendents need up-to-date data for decision-making.

Most offices will not send files that are patently outdated. Inactive letters are not usually discarded but rather kept in the file indefinitely, depending upon storage space limitations of the placement office.

Who should teaching candidates ask to write their letters of recommendation?

All references should be from persons in a supervisory capacity rather than from friends or peers. School administrators are interested in one's classroom performance. The reference letters must be original or contain an original (not photocopied) signature in order to verify their content.

How does an applicant go about sending a credentials file to a local school district?

Requests to send a file to a potential employing school district must be in writing. Processing time can be as long as two to three days in our office, but next day service is usually a goal. Candidates with last minute requests are advised to present an unofficial copy (their own) to the school district. Some placement offices will read the letters over the phone at the request of school officials. If a decision to hire is contemplated, the school administrator will then request an official copy from the placement office.

Are fees required?

Each placement office sets its own policy regarding fees for such services as credentials requests. With or without a fee structure, there is usually some limitation placed upon file usage.

Do school districts call the placement office?

Yes. School districts often call the placement office requesting help to fill a teaching position. Our staff will then match job requirements with those of active candidates and refer appropriate people. Referring qualified job applicants often happens close to the beginning of a new school year or term. It may happen because of an unexpected vacancy. Districts often request referrals for openings for which they have a limited number of candidates. Recently, for example, there have been many requests to assist districts in their search for substitute teachers.

When is hiring done?

Hiring occurs throughout the year but most openings are available at the beginning of the school year (August/September). Notices of projected openings begin to appear as soon as January. There has been a trend toward early recruitment of candidates. However, most districts do not know their exact openings (vacancies and teaching areas) until later in the spring.

In what subjects are you seeing shortages of qualified teachers?

Disciplines that are more likely to have job openings are the sciences, math, bilingual education, and behavior disorders. Areas of oversupply seem to be art, social studies, and physical education. But much depends on the geographic location in which you are seeking a position.

Exactly how important is geography in finding a teaching job?

It's very important. Growing population centers need more teachers than those with a shrinking school-age group. There is more likely to be stiff competition for jobs in desirable suburban areas than in more distant rural communities. Most urban, big city school districts are always seeking qualified teachers.

Besides geography, what other factors are influencing teacher supply and demand?'

Many items have to be considered. Teacher turnover and retirement, district or state-wide curriculum changes, and budget cutbacks or expansions are just a few. Today's teacher corps is an aging group, on the whole, and many are nearing retirement. This has come about because of the lack of education openings in the past decade. Conversely, many persons are reentering the teacher job market because it is growing and the opportunities outside of education are not as plentiful, and for some, not as rewarding as they had supposed. The number of new teacher candidates being prepared has decreased but this situation is changing as the word gets out that good jobs are available.

What about mid-year graduates?

There are fewer jobs in January and February; mid-year graduates face a tougher job market. They are advised to consider substituting in order to get experience and become known in districts in which they will be seeking a job. They should not limit themselves to public schools. Private and parochial schools should also be considered even though, as a rule, they offer lower salaries.

What are some of the major sources of information about education job vacancies?

Job applicants should remember to contact the principal and administrators where they student taught or did their clinical experience. These people know the staffing needs of their districts as well as the needs of administrators in neighboring schools.

Job boards and vacancy listings maintained by the college placement office are also excellent sources for finding teaching positions. Vacancies appear on the job board when the application deadline falls too close to a publication date or if the position is particularly attractive and bound to draw many candidates. The placement office wants its graduates to learn about the opening immediately.

Faculty can be another source of job openings, since they are often in touch with school administrators and learn about available positions before the word goes out to the general public.

Teacher placement days or fairs seem to be a growing trend across the country. What accounts for their popularity? What advice would you offer a candidate who attends one of these recruiting fairs?

Teacher fairs are becoming very prominent. They're extremely valuable; it's a "can't lose" experience for teachers and school districts alike. Applicants should look professional, have copies of their resume to hand out, and be prepared to present themselves and their qualifications in a very limited period of time. Remember that seeking a job is a sales situation. Convince the potential employer that you are the best candidate.

In a placement fair situation, candidates can also learn about school districts and openings they had not considered previously. Various colleges and universities host these events -- check with your placement office for details about upcoming teacher fairs. A growing number of school districts host an open house day where candidates get to meet administrators and teachers, tour the schools, and look over the community. Watch local bulletin boards for notices publicizing this popular recruitment event in your area.

The placement office does more than just match people to jobs. What other services does your office provide?

Besides the specific job related services I've already mentioned, our office arranges one-to-one career counseling (including personal interest inventories); a semester-long "Career and Life Planning" course; workshops to help decide on an academic major; personal growth and skill building classes; and student employment opportunities. We also maintain an alumni job network and repersonal growth and skill building classes; and student employment opportunities. We also maintain an alumni job network and resume pool. With regard to the resume pool, seniors and alumni register with the placement office and file their resumes for employer reviews and job-match referrals.

We critique resumes as well. Resumes submitted to the office are individually evaluated and given constructive feedback on form and content. At our office, this service usually takes three to five working days. On-campus interviews with employing school districts are scheduled throughout the year. Our computer interactive guidance system allows each student an individual evaluation of interests, values, skills, and education, followed by an exploration of occupations; there's also help in assembling and planning a job strategy.

As you can see, your local college placement office is a lot more than just a classified ad service for teachers. It can help design a solid foundation for the student's professional future.

The Job Fair

Teacher job fairs are rapidly becoming an integral part of the recruitment process in education. Local school districts are finding it advantageous to join together in a type of regional collective. Job fairs give the participating school districts the opportunity to publicize their career vacancies before a large pool of qualified applicants; you have the opportunity of meeting representatives from several school systems at one time. Ease of communication, reduced recruiting costs, and a more relaxed, informal atmosphere are some additional benefits schools and teachers enjoy when they go to the fair.

February through June are "fair" months used to staff vacancies for the new school year beginning in September. Major convention centers, hotels, and colleges are the usual sites for teacher fairs. Sometimes they are sponsored in conjunction with a cooperating college or university; other times, the districts will sponsor the event independently.

On the following pages, you'll find a list of over fifty teacher fairs and the name of the person to contact for current dates.

Regional Job Fair Contact Information

COLORADO

Educational Recruiting Fair
Western State College
Gunnison, Colorado
Contact: David Berilla
(303)943-3068

Spring Education
  Recruiting Fair
University of Colorado
Boulder, Colorado
Contact: Lynne Boyle
(303)492-7433

DELAWARE

University of Delaware
Contact: Linda Natter
(302)451-1231

DISTRICT OF COLUMBIA

Teacher Recruitment Day
University of the District
  of Columbia
Contact: Edwin Daniel
(202)282-7557

FLORIDA

Teacher
Florida State University
Tallahassee, Florida
Contact: Myrna Unger
(904)644-6431

ILLINOIS

Mid-America Teacher
  Placement Days
Illinois State University
Normal, Illinois
Contact: Parker Lawlis
(309)438-5635

INDIANA

Teacher Candidate
  Interview Day
University of Indianapolis
Indianapolis, Indiana
Contact: Paul Gabonay
(317)788-3296

IOWA

Midwest Overseas
  Recruiting Fair
University of Northern Iowa
Cedar Falls, Iowa
Contact: Margy Washut
  or Donald Wood
(319)273-2083

Teacher Interview Day
University of Northern Iowa
Cedar Falls, Iowa
Contact: Donald Wood
(319)273-2081

KANSAS

Kansas State University
  Teacher Job Fair
Kansas State University
Manhattan, Kansas
Contact: James Akin
(913)532-6508

Teacher Career Fair
Fort Hays State
  University
Hays, Kansas
Contact: Millie Schuster
(913)628-4260

Teacher Placement Day
University of Kansas
Lawrence, Kansas
Contact: Terry Glenn
(913)864-3624

Regional Job Fair Contact Information

MARYLAND

Education Job Fair
Towson State University
Towson, Maryland
Contact: Alice Feeney
(301)321-2233

MAASCUS/Maryland
   Metropolitan
   Area Teacher
   Interviewing
University of Maryland
College Park, Maryland
Contact: Marie Purcell
(301)454-4856

MASSACHUSETTS

Boston - Park Plaza
Contact: Floyd Martin
(413)545-2224

MICHIGAN

Career Fair
Western Michigan
   University
Kalamazoo, Michigan
Contact: Bonnie Truax
(616)383-1710

MINNESOTA

Minnesota Education Job Fair
St. Olaf College
Northfield, Minnesota
Contact: Forster Davis
(507)663-3268

Minnesota Job Fair
   (St. Paul)
Contact: Walt Larson
(612)255-2151

MISSOURI

Teacher Placement Day
Missouri Western State College
St. Joseph, Missouri
Contact: Lynn Compton
(816)271-4205

Teacher Placement Day
SW Missouri State
   University
Springfield, Missouri
Contact: Marlene Morrison
   or Allen MacDougall
(417)836-5636

MONTANA

Teacher Recruitment Week
Eastern Montana College
Billings, Montana
Contact: Larry Kannah
(406)657-2168

University of Montana
   Teachers Career Fair
University of Montana
Missoula, Montana
Contact: Don Hjelmseth
(406)243-2022

NEBRASKA

NASCUS Teacher Selection Day
Kearney State College
Kearney, Nebraska
Contact: Jackie Rosenlof
(308)234-8501

Teacher College Interview Fair
University of Nebraska
Lincoln, Nebraska
Contact: James Schiefelbein
(402)489-1897

Regional Job Fair Contact Information

NEW HAMPSHIRE

Education/Non-Profit Job Fair
New Hampshire College &
University
Manchester,
  New Hampshire
Contact: Pamela Ritchie
(603)669-3432

NEW JERSEY

Rutgers University - Hyatt
Contact: Glenn Gamble
(201)932-7287

NEW YORK

Central New York Teacher
  Recruitment
Syracuse University
  School of Education
Syracuse, New York
Contact: Marie Sarno
(315)423-2526

Suny Brockport
  (Rochester Area)
Contact: Gerald Wrubel
(716)245-5721

Teacher Recruitment Days
SUNY College
Buffalo, New York
Contact: Cecile Biltekoff
(716)878-5811

NORTH CAROLINA

Carolina Education Job Fair
University of
  North Carolina
Chapel Hill, North Carolina
Contact: Kathy Sack
(919)962-6507

Meredith Teacher Network
Meredith College
Raleigh, North Carolina
Contact:
  Mary Anna Newman
(919)829-8341

NORTH DAKOTA

University of North Dakota
Contact: (701)777-3904

OHIO

Education Expo/
Career Day
Cleveland State University
Cleveland, Ohio
Contact: Steve Kravinsky
(216)687-2246

Ohio State University
  (Columbus)
Contact: Pat Haynes
(614)292-2741

Malone College Annual Job Fair
Malone College
Canton, Ohio
Contact:
  Julie Ott or Gene George
(216)489-0800

Kent State University
Contact: Jerry Partyka
Career Planning/Placement
Kent, Ohio 44240
(216)672-2360

Teacher Recruitment
  Consortium
Rio Grande College
Rio Grande, Ohio
Contact:
  Margaret (Peg) Thomas
(614)245-5353

Regional Job Fair
Contact Information

Teacher Job Fair
Bowling Green State
  University
Bowling Green, Ohio
Contact: Louise Paradis
(419)372-2356

PENNSYLVANIA

Duquesne University
Contact: Carol Cantini
(412)434-6644

Mercyhurst College
Contact: John Gallo
(812)732-2781

Millersville
Contact:
  Dr. Frank Rozman
(717)872-3315

Slippery Rock University
Contact: Carla Hart
(412)794-7235

North Central Pennsylvania
  Education Consortium
Bloomsburg University
Bloomsburg, Pennsylvania
Contact: Carol Barnett
(717)389-4070

SOUTH CAROLINA

University of
  South Carolina
Contact: Linda Salane
(803)777-3166

TENNESSEE

Nashville Area Teacher
  Recruitment Week
Vanderbilt University
Nashville, Tennessee
Contact: Linda Bird
(615)322-3407

TEXAS

Angelo State University Annual
  Teacher Fair
Angelo State University
San Angelo, Texas
Contact: Jim Glassbrenner
(915)942-2255

Educational Interview Day
North Texas State
  University
Denton, Texas
Contact: Carolyn Bray
(817)565-2105

Educational Interview and
  Career Day
Texas Woman's University
Denton, Texas
Contact: Sue Cook
(817)898-2970

Teacher Career Day
University of Texas
El Paso, Texas
Contact: Briane Carter
(915)747-5640

Teacher Job Fair
Pan American University
Edinburg, Texas
Contact: Derly Guajardo
(512)381-2243

West Texas State
Contact:
  Gene Parker, Director
Career Planning/Placement
Box 728, W.T. Station
Canyon, Texas 79016

Regional Job Fair Contact Information

UTAH

Utah Teacher Fair
Utah State University
Logan, Utah
Contact: Paul Murray
(801)750-1747

WEST VIRGINIA

Teacher Recruitment
    Consortium
Marshall University
Huntington, West Virginia
Contact: Lind Oleson
(304)696-2370

West Virginia University
Contact: Robert Kent
(304)293-2221

WISCONSIN

Wisconsin Education
    Recruitment Fair
Contact: Tom Kelley
(608)262-1755

Local Hiring

Teaching jobs are local jobs.   Local school districts are autonomous administrative units in their hiring of teachers and other educational personnel; each one undertakes an independent evaluation of your application, resume, and credentials in relation to its own personnel needs.

Districts vary widely in size.   The largest districts serve hundreds of thousands of pupils and employ thousands of teachers, while the smaller districts may consist of a single school.   The geographic area of a school district may or may not coincide with the boundary of the cities, towns, and villages it serves.

States are divided into numerous local school districts; they range in number from a few dozen to several hundred. Hawaii and the District of Columbia are exceptions: they operate as single school district hiring units.

Here's a partial list of some of the larger school districts in the country.   If you're interested in working for one of these districts, you should contact the appropriate personnel office.   For a much more detailed look at the hiring picture nationwide, you may wish to consult *The Job Bank Guide To Education Employment,* also published by Bob Adams Inc. It features contact and certification information for thousands of school districts across the country.

In using this list, remember that a quick phone call to verify the district's current administrative address is always advisable.

Local District Contact Information

ALABAMA

Mobile County Public
  School System
Division of Human
  Resources
P.O. Box 1327
Mobile,
  Alabama 36604
(205)690-8083

Montgomery Public
  Schools
Personnel Department
307 South Decatur
P.O. Box 1991
Montgomery,
  Alabama 36197
(205)269-3000

ALASKA

Anchorage School
  District
Staffing Department
4600 De Barr Avenue
P.O. Box 196614
Anchorage, Alaska
  99519-6614
(907)333-9561

Fairbanks North Star
Borough School
  District
Personnel Department
Ninth and Cushman
  Streets
P.O. Box 1250
Fairbanks,
  Alaska 99707
(907)452-2000

ARIZONA

Phoenix Elementary
  School District 1
Personnel Department
125 East Lincoln
  Street
Phoenix, Arizona 85004
(602)257-3755

Tucson Unified
  School District 1
Personnel Department
P.O. Box 40400
1010 East Tenth Street
Tucson, Arizona 85719
(602)882-2400

ARKANSAS

Little Rock
  School District
Personnel Department
810 West Markham
Little Rock,
  Arkansas 72201
(501)374-3361

Texarkana School
  District 7
Personnel Department
3512 Grand Avenue
Texarkana,
  Arkansas 75502
(501)772-3371

CALIFORNIA

Los Angeles Unified
School District
Certificated Recruitment
  and Selection Section
Department Y
450 North Grand Avenue
Room C-102
Los Angeles,
  California 90012
(213)625-6356

Local District Contact Information

San Francisco Unified
School District
Certificated Personnel
  Services Division
135 Van Ness Avenue
Room 116
San Francisco,
  California 94102
(415)565-9256

COLORADO

Aurora Public Schools
Personnel Office
1085 Peoria Street
Aurora, CO 80011
(303)344-8060

Denver Public Schools
Department of Personnel
  Services
900 Grant Street
Denver, Colorado 80203
(303)837-1000

CONNECTICUT

Fairfield Public Schools
Personnel Department
P.O. Box 220
760 Stillson Road
Fairfield,
  Connecticut 06430
(203)255-8369

Hartford Public Schools
Office of Personnel &
  Labor Relations
249 High Street
Hartford,
  Connecticut 06103
(203)722-8525

DELAWARE

Caesar Rodney School
  District
Personnel Department
Old North Road
Box 188
Camden-Wyoming,
  Delaware 19934
(302)697-2173

Christina School
  District
Office of Personnel
  Services
83 East Main Street
Newark, Delaware 19711
(302)454-2000

DISTRICT OF COLUMBIA

District of Columbia
  Public Schools
Division of Human
  Resource Management
415 12th Street N.W.
Washington, D.C. 20004
(202)724-4080

FLORIDA

School Board/Broward
  County, Florida
Instructional Staffing
  Department
1320 SW Fourth Street
Fort Lauderdale,
  Florida 33310
(305)765-6170
(305)765-6161
  (Vacancy Hotline)

Local District Contact Information

Dade County
Public Schools
Bureau of Personnel
Management
1550 North Miami Avenue
Miami, Florida 33136
(305)372-5410

HAWAII

Hawaii State
Department of Education
Certificated Personnel
Management System
Office of Personnel
Services
1390 Miller Street
Room 310
P.O. Box 2360
Honolulu,
Hawaii 96804
(808)548-5297

IDAHO

Independent School
District of Boise
Personnel Office
1207 Fort Street
Boise,
Idaho 83702-5339
(208)338-3400

Twin Falls
School District 411
Personnel Department
201 Main Avenue West
Twin Falls,
Idaho 83301
(208)733-6900

ILLINOIS

Chicago Public Schools
Bureau of Teacher
Personnel
1819 West Pershing Road
Chicago, Illinois 60609
(312)890-7615

Springfield Public
School District 186
Personnel Department
1900 West Monroe
Springfield,
Illinois 62704
(217)525-3006

INDIANA

Indianapolis Public
Schools
Personnel Administration
Education Center
120 East Walnut Street
Indianapolis, Indiana
(317)266-4583

South Bend Community
School Corporation
Personnel Department
635 South Main Street
South Bend,
Indiana 46601
(219)282-4000

IOWA

Des Moines Public
Schools
Department of Personnel
1800 Grand Avenue
Des Moines,
Iowa 50307-3382
(515)242-7846

Local District
Contact Information

Iowa City Community
   School District
Personnel Department
509 South Dubuque Street
Iowa City, Iowa 52240
(319)338-3685

KANSAS

Topeka Unified
   School District 501
Personnel Department
624 South West 24th Street
Topeka, Kansas 66611
(913)233-0313

Wichita Public Schools
Division of
   Personnel Services
428 South Broadway
Wichita, Kansas 67202
(316)268-7817

KENTUCKY

Covington Independent
   School District
Personnel Department
25 East Seventh Street
Covington,
   Kentucky 41011
(606)292-5888

Jefferson County
   Public Schools
Personnel Services -
   Certified
3332 Newburg Road
P.O. Box 34020
Louisville,
   Kentucky 40232
(502)456-3114

LOUISIANA

East Baton Rouge
   Parish School Board
Personnel Department
1050 South Foster
P.O. Box 2950
Baton Rouge,
   Louisiana 70821
(504)926-2790

New Orleans Public
   Schools
Personnel Department
4100 Touro Street
New Orleans,
   Louisiana 70122
(504)286-2822

MAINE

Bangor School District
Personnel Department
435 Broadway Street
Bangor, Maine 04401
(207)947-7386

Portland Public Schools
Department of Personnel
331 Veranda Street
Portland, Maine 04103
(207)775-0900

MARYLAND

Baltimore City
   Public School System
Division of Human Resources
   and Labor Relations
3 East 25th Street
Baltimore,
   Maryland 21218
(301)396-6884

Local District Contact Information

Prince George's County
  Public Schools
Personnel Department
14201 School Lane
Upper Marlboro,
  Maryland 20722
(301)952-6180

MASSACHUSETTS

Boston Public Schools
Personnel Department
26 Court Street
Boston,
  Massachusetts 02108
(617)726-6600

Cambridge Public Schools
Personnel Department
159 Thorndike Street
Cambridge,
  Massachusetts 02141
(617)498-9247

MICHIGAN

Battle Creek
  Public Schools
Administration and
  Personnel
3 West Van Buren
Battle Creek,
  Michigan 49017-3079
(616)965-9468

Detroit Public Schools
Personnel Department
5057 Woodward
Detroit, Michigan 48202
(313)494-1862

MINNESOTA

Bloomington School
  District 271
Personnel Department
8900 Portland Avenue South
Bloomington,
  Minnesota 55420
(612)887-9123

Minneapolis Public Schools
Human Resources Department
807 Northeast Broadway
Minneapolis,
  Minnesota 55413-2398
(612)627-2032

MISSISSIPPI

Jackson Public
  School District
Office of Personnel
  Services
662 South President Street
Jackson, Mississippi 39205
(601)960-8745

Natchez Separate Municipal
  School District
Personnel Department
108 South Commerce Street
P.O. Box 1188
Natchez, Mississippi 39120
(601)442-0212

MISSOURI

Jefferson City
  Public Schools
Personnel Department
315 East Dunklin
Jefferson City,
  Missouri 65101
(314)636-7171

Local District Contact Information

St. Louis Public
  Schools
Personnel Office
911 Locust Street
St. Louis, Missouri 63101
(314)231-3720

MONTANA

Billings Public Schools
Personnel Department
101 Tenth Street West
Billings, Montana 59102
(406)248-7421

Helena School
  District No. 1
Personnel Department
402 North Warren
Helena, Montana 59601
(406)442-2590

NEBRASKA

Lincoln Public Schools
Personnel Department
720 South 22nd
Lincoln,
  Nebraska 68510
(402)475-1081

Omaha Public Schools
Department of Staff
  Personnel Services
3902 Davenport Street
Omaha, Nebraska 68131
(402)554-6216

NEVADA

Clark County
  School District
Personnel Department
2832 East Flamingo Road
Las Vegas, Nevada 89121
(702)799-5011

Washoe County
  School District
Personnel Department
425 East Ninth Street
Reno, Nevada 89520
(702)322-7041

NEW HAMPSHIRE

Manchester Union 37
Personnel Department
88 Lowell Street
Manchester,
  New Hampshire 03104
(603)624-6300

Portsmouth School
  Department
Personnel Department
Clough Drive
Portsmouth,
  New Hampshire 03801
(603)431-5080

NEW JERSEY

Newark Board of
  Education
Department of Human
  Resource Services
2 Cedar Street
Newark,
  New Jersey 07102-3091
(201)733-8760

Local District Contact Information

Trenton School District
Personnel Department
108 North Clinton Avenue
Trenton, New Jersey 08618
(609)989-2461

NEW MEXICO

Albuquerque Public Schools
Personnel Department
725 University Boulevard,
  Southeast
Box 25704
Albuquerque,
  New Mexico 87125
(505)842-3724

Santa Fe Public Schools
Personnel Department
610 Alta Vista Street
Santa Fe,
  New Mexico 87501
(505)982-2631, ext. 52

NEW YORK

New York City
  Public Schools
Division of Personnel
Office of Recruitment
  and Counseling
65 Court Street
Brooklyn,
  New York 11201
(718)935-2000

Rochester City
  School District
Teacher Personnel
  Office
131 West Broad Street
Rochester,
  New York 14608
(716)325-4560

NORTH CAROLINA

Burlington City Schools
Personnel Department
1712 Vaughn Road
Box 938
Burlington,
  North Carolina 27215
(919)226-1151

Wake County Public
  Schools System
Personnel Department
3600 Wake Forest Road
P.O. Box 28041
Raleigh,
  North Carolina 27611
(919)790-2596

NORTH DAKOTA

Bismarck Public
  School System
Personnel Department
400 Avenue E East
Bismarck, North Dakota
(701)221-3700

Grand Forks Public Schools
Personnel Department
308 De Mers
P.O. Box 6000
Grand Forks,
  North Dakota 58206-6000
(701)775-3111

OHIO

Cincinnati Public
  School District
Personnel Department
230 East Ninth Street
Cincinnati, Ohio 45202
(513)369-4820

Local District
Contact Information

Cleveland Public Schools
Division of Certificated
  Personnel
1380 East Sixth Street
Cleveland, Ohio 44114
(216)574-8000

OKLAHOMA

Oklahoma City
  Public Schools
Personnel Department
900 North Klein
Oklahoma City,
  Oklahoma 73106
(405)272-5520

Tulsa Public Schools
Division for Business and
  Personnel Services
3027 South New Haven
P.O. Box 470208
Tulsa, Oklahoma 74147
(701)221-3700

OREGON

Portland Public Schools
Personnel Services
501 North Dixon
Portland, Oregon 97227
(503)249-2000

Salem-Keizer School
  District 24 J
Personnel Department
1309 Ferry Street
  Southeast
Salem, Oregon 97309
(503)399-3061

PENNSYLVANIA

The School District
  of Philadelphia
Office of Personnel
  Operations
21st and Race Streets
Philadelphia,
  Pennsylvania 19103-1001
(215)299-8802

Pittsburgh Public Schools
Personnel Department
341 South Bellefield Avenue
Pittsburgh,
  Pennsylvania 15213
(412)622-3680

RHODE ISLAND

Cranston Public Schools
Personnel Department
845 Park Avenue
Cranston,
  Rhode Island 02910
(401)785-0400

Providence Public Schools
Personnel Department
211 Veazie Street
Providence,
  Rhode Island 02904
(401)456-9100

SOUTH CAROLINA

Charleston County
  School District
Division of Personnel
  Services
The Center, Meeting &
  Hutson Streets
Charleston,
  South Carolina 29403
(803)724-7711

Local District Contact Information

Lancaster County
  School District
Personnel Department
Drawer 130
Lancaster,
  South Carolina 29720
(803)285-1555

SOUTH DAKOTA

Rapid City
Area Schools 51-4
Personnel Department
809 South Street
Rapid City,
  South Dakota 57701
(605)394-4014

Sioux Falls School
  District 49-5
Personnel Office
201 East 38th Street
Sioux Falls,
  South Dakota 57117-5051
(605)331-7660

TENNESSEE

Knoxville City Schools
Personnel Department
101 East Fifth Avenue
Knoxville, Tennessee 37917
(615)544-3719

Memphis City Schools
Division of Employment
  and Placement
Room 164
2597 Avery Avenue
Memphis, Tennessee 38112
(901)454-5304

TEXAS

Dallas Independent
  School District
Human Resources Department
3700 Ross Avenue
Dallas, Texas 75204-5491
(214)824-1620

Houston Independent
  School District
Personnel Services Office
3830 Richmond Avenue
Houston, Texas 77027-5838
(713)623-5111

UTAH

Provo School District
Personnel Department
940 North 280 West
Provo, Utah 84604
(801)373-6301

Salt Lake City
  School District
Office of Personnel
  Services
440 East First South
Salt Lake City,
  Utah 84111
(801)328-7343

VERMONT

Burlington School
  District
Personnel Department
14 South Williams
Burlington,
  Vermont 05401
(802)864-8461

Local District Contact Information

Montpelier School
District
Personnel Department
58 Barre Street
Montpelier,
Vermont 05602
(802)223-6341

VIRGINIA

Chesterfield County
Public Schools
Department of
Instructional Personnel
P.O. Box 10
Chesterfield,
Virginia 23832
(804)748-1451

Norfolk Public Schools
Department of Personnel
800 East City Hall Avenue
Norfolk, Virginia 23510
(804)441-2717

WASHINGTON

Olympia School District
Personnel Department
1113 East Legion Way
Olympia, Washington 98501
(206)753-8900

Seattle Public Schools
Personnel Services
Department
815 Fourth Avenue North
Seattle, Washington 98109
(206)281-6663

WEST VIRGINIA

Greenbrier County Schools
Personnel Office
202 Chestnut Street
Lewisburg,
West Virginia 24901
(304)645-1260

Kanawha County Schools
Division of Personnel
200 Elizabeth Street
Charleston,
West Virginia 25311
(304)348-7770

WISCONSIN

Madison Metropolitan
School District
Personnel Department
545 West Dayton Street
Madison, Wisconsin 53703
(608)266-6058

Milwaukee School District
Personnel Department
5225 West Vliet Street
Milwaukee, Wisconsin 53201
(414)647-6200

WYOMING

Laramie County School
District #1
Personnel Department
2810 House Avenue
Cheyenne, Wyoming 82001
(307)632-0591. ext. 162

Local District Contact Information

Natrona County School
  District #1
Division of
  Personnel Services
970 North Glenn Road
Casper, Wyoming 82601
(307)237-9571

Get Involved!

Join an educational association in your field of interest and expertise soon after graduation. Professional organizations will not only assist in your job search by putting you in contact with fellow teachers and administrators -- they are also a virtual necessity for updating knowledge of students, methods, and materials once your career begins. You might contribute an article or research report to your association's journal or newsletter, or attend their regional or national conferences.

Here's a list of over 30 of the most prominent educational associations for elementary and high school teachers in the United States:

American Alliance for Health,
Physical Education,
Recreation, and Dance
1900 Association Drive
Reston, Virginia 22091
(703)476-3400

American Association for Gifted Children
15 Gramercy Park
New York, New York 10003
(212)473-4266

American Association of Physics Teachers
Graduate Physics Building
State University of New York
Stony Brook, New York 11794
(516)246-6840

American Federation of Teachers, AFL-CIO
11 DuPont Circle, NW
Washington, DC 20036
(202)797-4400

American Library Association
50 East Huron
Chicago, Illinois 60611
(312)944-6780

American Mathematical Society
201 Charles Street
P.O. Box 6248
Providence, Rhode Island 02940
(401)272-9500

American Montessori Society
150 Fifth Avenue
New York, New York 10011
(212)924-3209

American Personnel and Guidance Association
5203 Leesburg Pike
Falls Church, Virginia 22041
(703)820-4700

American School Counselor Association
(Division of the American Personnel and Guidance Association)
5203 Leesburg Pike
Falls Church, Virginia 22041
(703)820-4700

American Speech - Language - Hearing Association
10801 Rockville Pike
Rockville, Maryland 20852
(301)897-5700

Association for Childhood Education International
3615 Wisconsin Avenue, NW
Washington, DC 20016
(202)363-6963

Association for Counselor Education and Supervision
(Division of the American Personnel and Guidance Association)
5203 Leesburg Pike
Falls Church, Virginia 22041
(703)820-4700

Association of Teacher Educators
1900 Association Drive
Suite ATE
Reston, Virginia 22091
(703)620-3110

Council for Advancement and Support of Education
11 Dupont Circle, NW
Suite 400
Washington, DC 20036
(202)328-5900

Council for Children With Behavioral Disorders
c/o Council For Exceptional Children
1920 Association Drive
Reston, Virginia 22091
(800)336-3728

Council for Elementary Science International
1742 Connecticut Avenue, NW
Washington, DC 20009
(202)328-5810

Council for Exceptional Children
1920 Association Drive
Reston, Virginia   22091
(703)620-3660

Music Educators National Conference
1902 Association Drive
Reston, Virginia   22091
(703)860-4000

Music Teachers National Association
2113 Carew Tower
Cincinnati, Ohio   45202
(513)421-1420

National Art Education Association
1916 Association Drive
Reston, Virginia   22091
(703)860-8000

National Association for Bilingual Education
1201 16th Street, NW
Washington, DC   20036
(202)833-4271

National Association for Business Teacher Education
1914 Association Drive
Reston, Virginia   22091
(703)860-0213

National Association for the Education of Young Children
1834 Connecticut Avenue, NW
Washington, DC   20009
(202)232-8777

National Association of Biology Teachers, Inc.
11250 Roger Bacon Drive
Suite 19
Reston, Virginia   22090
(703)471-1134

National Association of Industrial and
   Technical Teacher Educators
103 Industrial Education
University of Missouri
Columbia, Missouri   65211
(314)882-3082

National Business Education Association
1914 Association Drive
Reston, Virginia   22091
(703)860-0213

National Council for the Social Studies
3615 Wisconsin Avenue, NW
Washington, DC   20016
(202)966-7840

National Council of Teachers of English
1111 Kenyon Road
Urbana, Illinois   61801
(217)328-3870

National Council of Teachers of Mathematics
1906 Association Drive
Reston, Virginia   22091
(703)620-9840

National Education Association
1201 16th Street, NW
Washington, DC   20036
(202)833-4000

National Science Teachers Association
1742 Connecticut Avenue, NW
Washington, DC   20009
(202)328-5800

National Vocational Guidance Association
(Division of the American Personnel
and Guidance Association)
5203 Leesburg Pike
Falls Church, Virginia   22041
(703)820-4700

School Science and Mathematics Association, Inc.
Indiana University of Pennsylvania
P.O. Box 1614
Indiana, Pennsylvania   15705

Speech Communication Association
5105 Blacklist
Suite E
Annandale, Virginia   22003
(703)750-0533

Saying "No" to Rejection

Rejection is part of the employment process. It may occur in your initial attempts to secure a teaching position within a particular school or school district; it may occur years later as you move up the career ladder and apply for jobs in educational consulting or school administration. Handling rejection with confidence and self-esteem must be an integral part of your total job search strategy.

People who never worry about being rejected for a job are those who never try. If you need a 100% guaranteed procedure for the complete avoidance of rejection, here it is:

NEVER ATTEMPT TO ACCOMPLISH ANYTHING.

The above advice constitutes the only foolproof (some might say "foolish") method for actually conquering rejection. However, if this technique is impractical for you (and it should be), then it's best to simply confront rejection as another task in your education job hunt. Getting state certified, writing resumes, calling school districts, filling out forms, interviewing, and coping with rejection are all unavoidable parts of a course of action that will put you in a rewarding and satisfying classroom position.

Job rejection is only a temporary, minor inconvenience. By maintaining a full schedule of job seeking activities, you'll have little time to worry about a rejection letter or two. Also, be aware that at some point in the job search process *you* may be the one doing the rejecting. If you apply to several school districts simultaneously (as many teachers do) and more than one offer of employment results, you'll be in a position to make a choice. And unfortunately, once you do, *one* of the districts is going to have to do without your services! (Who said life is fair?)

Here's a chart that lists some of the most frequent reasons teachers are rejected for jobs, along with a possible solution for each:

REASON FOR REJECTION	SOLUTION
Budget cutbacks, less tax revenue	Reapply every three months
Incomplete credentials file	Complete all parts of application forms; resubmit
Inappropriate state certificate	Obtain correct state certificate; reapply
Poor interview	Research school district and its policies thoroughly
Inexperienced	Apply for beginning-level teaching jobs
Too many applicants in one teaching area	Obtain additional state certificates
No full-time positions currently available.	Substitute

CHAPTER SUMMARY

Effective resumes and cover letters are major components in your job search; they'll help open the door to an interview.

Follow customary business guidelines and formats in writing your resume and cover letters.

Register early with your college placement office to take advantage of their complete range of job search materials.

Your individual job strategy includes both personal and professional acquaintances as well as a wide variety of resources.

Attend upcoming teacher recruitment fairs in your area; they are valuable placement methods for school districts and applicants alike.

Substitute work is an excellent beginning step toward full-time employment.

Don't wait for the "perfect" teaching situation; accept an offer of a permanent job position rather than continue working as a substitute.

Finding a job in education requires initiative, energy, and activity; it encompasses many situations that only occur outside of your house.

Limit all paperwork connected with your job search to evenings and weekends.

Join an educational association in your subject; participate in its meetings and contribute to its publications.

Job rejection is a temporary, minor inconvenience that is part of every professional job search.

Four:
Into the Interview

Research The District

Once you've received your state teaching certificate, submitted application forms and documents to several school districts, passed all the necessary competency tests, and conducted a thorough job search -- what's next? When your resume and application attract the interest of a personnel officer, you will be invited to visit the district. Interviewing is next on the job seeker's agenda.

Even though some nervousness is to be expected, don't be frightened at the thought of an interview. After all, teachers spend most of their careers giving group presentations and answering questions. You now possess the knowledge and ability to be successful under actual teaching conditions. (Remember student teaching?) There's nothing to worry about in a job interview -- as long as you are prepared.

Prepare for your interview just as you prepared for each of your college classes: research. Research everything you can about teaching in the school district you'll be visiting. Such effort may seem obvious, but unfortunately, many job candidates in education fail to do their homework. With that in mind, here are some "assignments" that should get you off to an excellent start in your personal interview:

Call or visit the district office several days prior to your interview. Obtain all the printed material (pamphlets, booklets, guides, fact sheets, etc.) that acquaints prospective teachers with the educational programs and working conditions in the school district.

Know the basic demographics of the district. What are its geographic boundaries? How many students are enrolled? What grade levels are served? How many teachers are employed? What grade levels are served?

Study statistics of pupil achievement in reading and math. Are most of the district's students below grade level? at grade level? above grade level?

Drive through the district. Acquaint yourself with

the students' socio-economic environment.

Review the district's directory of organization. Memorize some of the key names -- superintendent, personnel manager, head of curriculum. (These "names" may be conducting the interview.)

Visit a school. (Always call first for an appointment.) Talk to the teachers and administrators. Find out the major textbook series being utilized in the district, observe the professional staff's manner of dress, inquire about current district teacher training programs.

Research your possible work environment -- ask if the district's teachers are represented by a union. If yes, get a copy of the union contract and study the contractual agreements between the teachers' union and the school district.

Obtain a salary schedule from the district. (Avoid asking salary questions during the interview; salary is based on seniority and awarded degrees.)

Determine whether the district has a residency requirement. If you are applying to such a district, you should already be a resident or have plans to become one shortly after hiring.

Familiarize yourself with the district's instructional programs and learning objectives for its students.

Learn whether the district has received any special honors or recognition by state or federal agencies for academic excellence.

Find out what extra-curricular and sports programs are offered in the district.

If this seems like a lot of work -- it is! And it should be done for each school district that grants you an interview. But don't fret. All this detailed effort is worthwhile. It provides you with valuable job information. You'll see firsthand how different school districts compare in salary, professional opportunities, fringe benefits and working conditions. You'll be compiling your own teacher's job resource library, brimming with school districts' brochures, pamphlets, charts, directories and other documents. You'll be meeting key people at the district level -- principals and fellow teachers -- and developing future contacts. You'll also be coming very close to your final goal: a teaching assignment.

A Day Before the Interview You Should...

...drive or use public transportation to make a practice trip to the district office. Leave at the same time and follow the same route that you plan for the day of the interview. Become familiar with the roads and traffic. Allow at least an extra 30 minutes travel time on the appointment date. Be prompt!

...gather all the requested documents. They should be complete, accurate and neat. Bring duplicate copies of your application, resume and supporting forms even if the personnel office has them on file. Use a small zipper notebook for the forms. Organization is the mark of a professional.

...select the clothes you'll wear. By researching the district you will observe how other candidates and teachers dress for work. Project a well-groomed, polished image.

...review all the school district's brochures and pamphlets. Memorize key names from their directory of organization. Study systemwide programs, policies and objectives.

...rehearse answers to anticipated questions, especially any questions that appeared on the application for employment. Tape your responses and review them. Are they knowledgeable, direct and brief? Avoid slang expressions. Use proper English.

...prepare one or two structured questions of your own. You could be asked for comments and questions at the conclusion of the interview.

...be positive, confident and optimistic. You're in a no-lose situation. You win if a job offer soon arises from the interview. Even without an offer of employment you will have gained valuable experience and still might be employed by that district at a later date.

Interview Time

Teaching candidates confront two separate yet interrelated interviews -- a preliminary screening interview and a full-scale professional evaluation interview that produces the most apprehension. Be prepared for the school district's initial screening. You must be successful in the preliminary interview to continue on as a viable applicant.

In order to establish a pool of the most qualified teachers available, the district's personnel department will schedule you for the preliminary screening interview. The purpose of this interview is to review your supporting documents to ascertain that they meet minimum hiring guidelines. Among the items to be checked are:

State teaching certificate

NTE scores (if applicable)

Results of state/local competency tests (if applicable)

References

College transcripts

Grade point average

Local school district application

Prior teaching experience, including student teaching

Police background check

Medical examination

The personnel director or an assistant will review your file to determine that: your state teaching certificate is appropriate to the position applied for; your NTE scores, test results and G.P.A. meet or exceed district standards; your references are excellent or superior; your application form is complete, without any gaps in your employment history; your police record is negative; your medical examination is satisfactory; and that your other documents are in order and on file.

Based upon a recommendation generated from that initial document screening conference, you will then be invited for a second interview -- the full-scale professional evaluation. This interview, again conducted by the personnel department, will now include principals, curriculum specialists and other representatives of the district experienced in hiring decisions. Although teachers are not usually on the interview committee, remember that most principals and curriculum specialists were once classroom instructors. Be prepared for specific questions on your classroom philosophy and technique. Expect the committee to have from three to seven members.

First impressions are crucial. Your first few minutes can make a great deal of difference in a final hiring decision. Why? Consider the logistics of interviewing from the other side. A few people will be questioning a great many applicants within a short time. Most interviews are 30 minutes or less. It's easy for names, faces, questions and answers to become blurred after several hours and days of interviewing. With that knowledge, focus on your task: *Convince the evaluation committee through word and record of your sincerity in choosing teaching for a career and of your technical proficiency to be a teacher.*

Begin with a firm handshake. Firm handshakes are impressive, weak ones are not. Exemplify poise and self-assuredness by maintaining eye contact throughout the interview. Good posture is important - no slouching.

Speak up, too! Articulate your replies in a distinct and clear voice that's loud enough for everyone in the conference room to hear. Avoid a dull, soft monotone speech pattern that will either put the committee to sleep or keep them asking, "Would you please repeat that?"

Don't be afraid of using limited controlled body gestures. Hand movements or a change of facial expressions can emphasize your responses. After all, a teacher is expected to be an animated, dynamic instructional leader of children.

Warm, friendly, open, dedicated, earnest, hard-working and professional are traits the interviewers want to see reflected by your answers and attitude. Project those traits. Understand who is on the committee and what each member is looking for.

The Cast of Characters:

Personnel representative: concerned with written school board policy and your reaction to it.

Curriculum specialist: quizzes knowledge of methods, materials and theory in your teaching area.

Principal: interested in your ideas regarding common teaching situations and a variety of educational issues.

You are also being evaluated as a potential team player. Teaching is never viewed as an isolated assignment; quality education is the result of a cooperative undertaking between fellow teachers, administrators, support staff, children, parents and the community at large.

Appreciate the interview as a career opportunity in and of itself. Above all, just be yourself.

What Will They Ask?

Interview questions fall into four basic groups:

Subject Area Questions -- questions designed to test your knowledge of current theory/practice in your area of expertise (certification). They are usually asked by one of the district's curriculum specialists.

Personnel Department Questions -- questions to determine whether you will follow the rules and regulations of the school district. They are usually asked by a member of the personnel department.

Educational Methodology Questions -- questions to elicit your individual techniques in dealing with a variety of classroom situations. They are usually asked by a school principal.

Philosophy of Education/Teaching Questions -- questions to focus on your value system and committment to teaching. They may be asked by any member of the interview committee.

Answers should be:

Brief...   interviews are less than 30 minutes.

Direct...   respond to the questions.

Specific...   give examples from your background and training; do not talk in generalities.

Honest...   if you do not know the answer to a question, say so.

In speaking, reply to all the people present at the interview, not just the person asking the question. There should not by any "trick" questions in the interview. The committee is busy with many applicants. They'll give you straightforward questions and expect straightforward answers.

And, perhaps most important, *THINK CHILDREN* throughout the interview. Relate as many of your answers as possible to serving the educational and emotional needs of children. The questions that follow are representative samples only; you could be asked something entirely different in your interview. The first two questions in each area are accompanied by possible responses, to give you an idea of how an effective approach to the question can present you in the best possible light. While a number of questions have been reproduced below, anticipate only one or two questions from each category due to time limitations.

Subject Area Questions

Name and discuss a critical issue in your area of teaching.

Being an elementary math teacher, I believe the role of pocket calculators in the classroom is a basic issue -- one that remains unresolved even today. I definitely feel calculators are useful teaching aids that frequently help to motivate students to do their work. However, I wouldn't want my class to have to rely solely on a calculator in order to complete an assignment. Calculators must be strategically integrated into the overall math curriculum so that they support a pupil's instructional program, not supplant it.

How do you view your subject in relation to the total school curriculum?

Reading is fundamental to success in school. I know every teacher thinks that his or her subject area is the most important one, but without reading, students can do nothing. All the progress in other disciplines must wait when a child has failed to master comprehension, word attack, and vocabulary skills for their particular grade level. Reading is what school is all about. In fact, to me, reading is synonymous with school.

Cite two innovations in your field that interest you and tell us why.

What are some current methods and textbooks in your subject area?

Do you have any special or advanced training in your field?

What are your strengths and weaknesses in teaching your subject?

What do you feel should be the main curriculum components in your subject area?

Why did you decide to teach this subject?

Personnel Department Questions

Why do you want to teach in our school district?

I'm an educator, a community resident, and a taxpayer. Those are three reasons I have for wanting to teach here and see our students succeed. We must have productive schools and hard-working students, teachers, and parents if our region is going to continue to flourish. I want to make my own contribution, and after completing four years of teacher training, I couldn't think of anyplace where I'd rather make that contribution than right here at home.

Will you accept any assignment for which you are certified in our district's schools?

Definitely -- yes. I'm very adaptable regarding particular assignments within the school building. Of course, just like other teachers, I have a personal preference for a certain grade level and subject area within that grade. If I have a choice -- if I'm asked, that is -- I'll state my preference. Otherwise, I'd gladly accept any assignment on my certificate. I want to be a team member who is part of, not apart from, the district's faculty.

Are you interviewing with other school districts?

Will you take additional after-school training necessary for instruction if you do not currently have the preparation to teach in our district?

133

Will you attend after-school parent meetings, professional conferences and extra-curricular student activities?

Do you have any objection to supervising hall, lunchroom or playground activities during school hours?

Do you plan to further your education at a local college or university?

What community activities or organizations are you participating in?

Educational Methodology Questions

Given the choice, how and what would you report to parents about pupil progress?

I would use the standard district report cards to formally notify parents of their child's progress. However, in my judgment, report cards are issued too far apart, usually at 10-week intervals. Being a parent myself, I wouldn't want to wait two and a half months to see a progress report about my child. As a teacher, I would send weekly personalized notes or letters to my students' homes. In this manner, the official report card won't be a great shock -- pleasant or unpleasant. Also, by maintaining frequent parent contact, I'll be able to enlist cooperation in any problem areas. And I'll help the students to achieve more than I could by myself.

As for what I would report, it would be a combination of grades for academic subjects and comments based upon my classroom observation of a student's social adjustment or attitude. Both areas are so interrelated I couldn't grade one without the other. I would also include in my reports a student's attendance and tardiness record, and any special learning problems that I notice interfering with a pupil's overall progress.

How would you help a student who is having difficulty learning in your class?

There's a variety of methods I would employ in this situation. First, I would review the student's cumulative school record. Past learning history often provides clues as to present academic problems. Then, I would note if the problem is an isolated one, in one subject area, or if it's more generalized. A pupil who is doing well in all subjects except one may just need a little individual tutoring and encouragement to increase motivation. However, if the problem appears more widespread, it could indicate a physical impairment -- perhaps the child needs glasses or a hearing aid, or has a learning disability like dyslexia. I would, under those circumstances, consult with the school nurse or learning disabilities resource teacher. Classroom teachers who instructed the child in previous years, or who are currently teaching him or her in different classes, may be able to offer suggestions. I would definitely inform the student's parents of the problem -- as well as of every procedure I'm utilizing to correct it. And, of course, I would ask them for their comments or advice.

What would a visitor to your classroom see that would indicate that your instructional program is meeting the needs of individual students?

How would you manage your classroom? Describe your general discipline procedures.

How would you arrange children for the learning process? What grouping procedures would you employ?

How would you find out about students' attitudes and feelings regarding your class?

Philosophy of Education/Teaching Questions

What are your professional goals?

Right now, my main goal is to be the best possible teacher of U.S. history that I can. To achieve that end, I'm working at night on my Master's degree in history. I'm also enrolled in two evening workshops on topics related to the Civil War. I plan on diligently reading all the school district's bulletins and announcements for upcoming seminars in my subject area. I may even enroll in a few teaching workshops not in my subject area just to keep current on new developments. I also want to contribute to the professional journals that help teachers of U.S. history. In fact, I just submitted an article to The Social Studies Professional *on how sixth-grade teachers can make studying the Civil War more relevant; I'm waiting to see if it will be published. Eventually, I might want to train other teachers in methods of teaching American history -- or even go into school administration as a principal. But that's a long way into the future. Presently, all my professional goals are centered around classroom teaching and improving my own knowledge of United States history.*

Why will you be a good teacher?

I'll be a good listener -- I believe a good teacher must first be a good listener. For example, I would be careful to listen to more experienced teachers and to school officials, and to remain open to new ideas and suggestions -- even suggestions from students. Yet, at the same time, I'm my own person, a teacher with definite plans and methods that I expect to bring to the classroom. I'm adaptable to the variety of situations I know I'll encounter in teaching, from structured lessons to assembly rehearsals, and from parent teacher conferences to fire drills. I think I possess the confidence and maturity to handle any situation that arises, always keeping the well-being of my students foremost in mind. I want to contribute my skills and talents because I love the challenge of helping young people grow into independent adults. There's no greater challenge or occupation in the world than teaching.

Describe your personal philosophy of teaching.

Describe what you think is an ideal teacher-pupil relationship.

How do children learn?

What do you think provides the greatest pleasure in teaching?

What is your perception as to the future of public education?

Describe an effective teacher.

Follow Up

Shortly after the meeting with the professional evaluation committee, you will be notified in writing of their decision.   The outcome is usually stated in these terms with one box being checked:

☐   *Highly recommended for employment*

☐   *Recommended for employment*

☐   *Not recommended for employment*

Some school districts use a numerical ranking system instead.

If the committee voted against your eligibility, ask the personnel department for details.   Work on those areas of deficiency and reapply to the district during their next screening period.   You are, of course, free to apply to other school districts during this time.

If the interview resulted in a recommendation to hire, you still must wait. The committee's recommendation places your name on the district's eligibility list.   You'll be notified when vacancies occur in your area of state certification. The personnel department still takes into account several criteria, besides the interview, before a definite offer of employment is made and a contract offered. In staffing, they must also consider:

Education and training
Experience
Special abilities/talents
Credentials, including student teaching
Character
Health
Requirements of available position

Send a brief personal note of thanks to each committee member after your interview.   Thank them for their time and effort in evaluating your application for employment. At this point, once you've conveyed your solid preparation for the interview, cross your fingers and move on to the next district on your target list. Interview success, in combination with a specific job vacancy and other factors of education and experience, equals the start of a new teaching career -- yours.

CHAPTER SUMMARY

A personal interview at the school district's administrative office is an important part of the hiring process in education.

Thoroughly research each school district that schedules you for an interview.

There are several final areas of preparation that should be completed a day or two before the interview.

The interview may actually be two interviews -- a preliminary screening interview and a full-scale professional evaluation interview.

Your documentation for a teaching position is reviewed at the initial screening conference, while the professional evaluation interview is concerned with your technical competency and your choice of teaching as a career.

First impressions are vital considering the logistics of the interview process.

Each member of the interview committee questions you from their own perspective.

Interview answers should be brief, direct, specific and honest.

THINK CHILDREN during the interview.

Follow-up each interview on a positive note with thank you letters to the committee members.

Interview success combined with a specific job vacancy and other factors of education and experience equals an offer of employment by the school district.

Five:
On the Job

Teaching Contracts

A contract in education is a written agreement between the local school district and the individual teacher regarding the conditions of employment. Carefully read all parts of your contract before signing. Once signed by both parties, the contract is legally enforceable through our judicial system. Monetary damages can be assessed if you or the school district breach any of the contract's terms.

Teaching contracts are typically written for a period of one full calendar year beginning in September and ending the following August. By using a yearly contract, the school board maintains control and flexibility in the areas of staffing and salary. If tax revenues meet or exceed its requirements, the board will fund more positions and offer higher salary schedules. When tax revenues decline, job cutbacks and few if any salary increases can be expected.

The following pages feature an example of a teaching contract that may be in your future.

EMPLOYMENT AGREEMENT

LINCOLN SCHOOL DISTRICT #15 (hereinafter referred to as "the District") and _____ (hereinafter referred to as "the Teacher") mutually agree this _____ day of _____, 19____, on the following terms and conditions which shall, together with the policies and procedures of the district, be considered the Contract of Employment.

THE PRIMARY PURPOSE OF THIS AGREEMENT is to establish a working atmosphere with recognized mutual duties and responsibilities in order to provide quality education. Accordingly, each teacher will conduct himself/herself, both in the classroom and outside, as an exemplary citizen. Classes will be conducted pursuant to, and in a manner consistent with, the PHILOSOPHY, POLICIES, AND PROCEDURES of the district.

ARTICLE I -- COMPENSATION

Salary: for basic academic services (classes, etc.)

First Semester	$9,000
Second Semester	$9,000
Other Compensation:	
Track Coach	$1,500
TOTAL COMPENSATION	**$19,500**

Salary shall be paid on a semi-monthly basis less deductions required by law or authorized by the teacher.

The teacher shall be entitled to a maximum of 10 personal and/or sick days absence each year for bona fide sickness or personal absence without loss of pay.

The teacher may elect to receive the insurance benefits provided by the group hospitalization plan offered by the district by completion of required forms.

ARTICLE II - STATUS

Both the district and the teacher recognize that their rights and obligations are exclusively subject to and governed by provisions of the policies of Lincoln School District #15.

An administrator shall periodically review each teacher's classroom performance. Following the first 3 months of school, the administrator will have a private conference with each teacher. A written evaluation shall be prepared with a copy to the teacher, who shall have an opportunity to file a response in the personnel file.

The teacher shall be required to meet state certification and degree requirements for public school teachers. In addition, she/he shall demonstrate annually, in a manner satisfactory to the district, that she/he has advanced professionally through professional reading, or by participation in seminars, workshops, classes or other programs. Each teacher who does not possess a Master's Degree is strongly urged to pursue studies toward that end.

ARTICLE III – GRIEVANCE PROCEDURE

In the event of any dispute, the teacher may submit a grievance on a form provided by the district within either 5 calendar days from the date of the occurrence giving rise to the grievance, or 5 days from the date the teacher or district could reasonably have been expected to have knowledge of the occurrence. A grievance meeting shall be conducted within 10 days following the filing of the grievance between the principal, the teacher, and necessary witnesses. The principal must make known his or her decision within 5 days following the meeting. In the event that the grievant is dissatisfied with the principal's decision, the matter may be appealed to the Board of Trustees/Education Committee by written notice to the President of the Board within 5 calendar days following the decision. At least two representatives will be selected by the President from this committee. The representatives shall meet with the principal, teacher and the necessary witnesses. The committee shall render a decision within 5 days after meeting with the parties concerned.

ARTICLE IV – SPECIFIC OBLIGATIONS

The teacher agrees to be in school at 8:00 a.m. and in the classroom ready to commence the normal school day at 8:15 a.m. The teacher shall remain in her/his classroom until 3:00 p.m. and shall be present at reasonable times before and/or after the school day as required by the school for attendance at faculty, departmental and in-service meetings and workshops, counseling students, and/or parent interviews.

The normal program for a full-time teacher shall consist of twenty-five (25) class periods and five (5) professional preparation periods per week. The teacher's duties shall include emergency substitution duties, assigning and recording grades, care and responsibility of instructional equipment, supervision of students inside and outside the classroom, and presence at all assemblies where the teacher will be seated with her/his homeroom. Teachers, within their departments, are required to involve students in city or state- wide competition each school year. The teachers shall utilize books and instructional materials required by the school in the performance of her/his duties.

ARTICLE V - CONTRACT RENEWAL

This agreement shall not be automatically renewed every year. The renewal of this agreement shall be initiated as follows:

The district with the recommendation of the principal shall send a letter to the teacher on or before May 1, inquiring as to whether the teacher is interested in renewing his/her contract; the teacher shall respond indicating, "Yes, I am interested in renewal" or "No, I am not interested in renewal." The teacher shall respond in writing within 7 days from receipt of the district's letter. The letter shall be deemed received by the teacher when it is placed in the teacher's mailbox in the school. The letter from the district and a "yes" response from the teacher shall not constitute an agreement to renew. After receipt of a "yes" response from the teacher, the district may at its discretion offer a contract to the teacher for the following school year.

ARTICLE VI -- TERMS OF CONTRACT

This agreement may be amended only by mutually written consent of the parties.

The term of this contract shall be for one school year, commencing September 1, 19__, and terminating August 31, 19__.

AGREEMENT

District Superintendent

Principal

Teacher

Individual contracts are not usually offered in large city school districts. Instead, a joint agreement between the board of education and the teachers union governs all aspects of employment. You are not required to sign a separate contract in this instance, but must adhere to all the rules and regulations stipulated in the formal agreement issued by the district and local teachers union.

These documents are extensive; they cover hundreds of pages, take months to negotiate, involve many people on both sides, and provide a comprehensive framework for your teaching career. They constitute the final word on a great many issues, including: teacher assignment procedures and work load; class size; discipline policies; summer school; salaries, insurance, fringe benefits and related items; and promotional, evaluational, and transfer procedures.

Regardless of whether you plan on teaching in a large urban school or a smaller rural environment, it's best to obtain a copy of the written contract prior to your employment. Study all of the provisions, even down to the subsections and subparagraphs; be certain you intend to abide by them before you enter the classroom.

Nationwide Salary Survey

Let's talk money.

Fortunately, there's beginning to be something to talk about. In bygone eras, it was considered undignified for teachers to be concerned with such mundane matters as salaries and benefits. Nowadays, pay schedules are definitely improving as school boards nationwide finally recognize the fact that in order to attract quality teachers, districts must offer salaries competitive with pay in other professions.

Several states, as part of educational reform legislation, are in the process of mandating minimum salary levels; a figure of $20,000 is frequently mentioned as an acceptable base pay for new teachers. Teacher shortages in many areas are also helping to focus public attention on the need to improve salary levels in education.

The following chart of forty-two public school districts reflects salary ranges through the 1987 school year. The low end of the range (in the left-hand column) represents levels for new teachers without experience, while the top figures (on the right) are what an experienced teacher with an advanced degree (Master's or Doctorate) can expect to earn.

As you study this chart, remember: teachers are paid on the basis of a *ten-month* academic year.

Salary Levels: Selected Districts

District	Low	High
Anchorage, AK	$26,078	$52,646
Baltimore, MD	$17,000	$33,147
Boise, ID	$12,836	$30,891
Casper, WY	$18,600	$37,700
Charlestown, WV	$15,631	$29,016
Charleston County, SC	$10,281	$33,541
Chicago, IL	$17,651	$37,517
Cleveland, OH	$17,678	$37,457
Dallas, TX	$19,000	$31,000
Denver, CO	$16,882	$41,600
Des Moines, IA	$15,100	$30,351
Ft. Lauderdale, FL	$17,400	$32,281
Grand Forks, ND	$16,400	$32,941
Hartford, CT	$21,800	$45,500
Hawaii (entire state)	$17,607	$34,334
Houston, TX	$19,100	$33,180
Indianapolis, IN	$15,850	$33,721
Jackson, MS	$15,925	$28,175
Los Angeles, CA	$20,298	$37,679
Louisville, KY	$15,314	$30,781
Memphis, TN	$17,550	$33,175
Minneapolis, MN	$17,418	$41,809
Mobile, AL	$19,955	$26,257
Newark, NJ	$19,000	$36,876
New Orleans, LA	$16,032	$26,210

Salary Levels: Selected Districts

(continued)

District	Low	High
New York, NY	$20,000	$40,700
Norfolk, VA	$18,500	$33,070
Omaha, NE	$16,850	$33,700
Philadelphia, PA	$16,640	$38,498
Portland, ME	$14,500	$28,275
Portland, OR	$17,050	$33,248
Salt Lake City, UT	$15,180	$31,351
San Diego, CA	$19,357	$39,810
San Francisco, CA	$21,175	$36,995
Seattle, WA	$16,087	$33,485
Sioux Falls, SD	$13,850	$30,438
St. Louis, MO	$19,097	$36,680
Tucson, AZ	$19,976	$33,051
Tulsa, OK	$16,163	$32,326
Virginia Beach, VA	$18,404	$32,494
Wichita, KS	$17,000	$28,724

Summer School and Beyond: The Secrets of Extra Pay

A wide variety of methods exist for you to earn additional compensation. Here are some of the most popular:

Summer School: Don't wait until June to inquire about summer teaching positions in your district. Begin researching opportunities for summer classroom jobs shortly after the New Year begins. For further ideas, you may wish to consult the *Summer Employment Directory,* available through Writer's Digest Books or at your local library. You have at least two "free" months at your disposal -- use them to generate extra income!

Advanced degrees. Obtain your advanced degree as soon as possible -- it's the single most important way to improve your salary level. Even if the scheduled difference between a teacher with a Bachelor's degree and one with a Master's degree may be only $1,000, that can add up. If you multiply that $1,000 (and the interest that would accompany it) by each year of your teaching career, you'll soon realize that tens of thousands of dollars are at stake.

Curriculum writing. Many school districts recruit their own teachers to revise curriculum guides and prepare other instructional materials.

In-service workshops. Teachers who develop particular areas of skill or expertise may be asked to give presentations at in-service meetings.

After-school activities. An entirely new world of school functions begins when the final bell rings. Among the most likely income-enhancing activities are: coaching an athletic team; evaluating textbooks (perhaps through an already existing committee); sponsoring a club; editing a newspaper or yearbook; heading a (previously) unorganized department; and assisting "problem" students in other classes if your background warrants this.

"But most of these activities are unpaid," you may be saying to yourself. True. Many jobs or activities that earn teachers additional pay did not begin as part of a job description. Faculty members freely donated their time without regard to salary. Later, the school board decided to institute compensation programs for those extra-curricular activities. Remember how you made sure to "think children" during your job interview? That kind of thinking doesn't stop when you acquire a position. If nothing else, working in the areas outlined above will enhance your standing as a "kids-first" team player. That doesn't hurt.

So -- don't wait for the job. Do it. The rewards will come later.

The Benefits Package

Salaries and opportunities for additional pay are only part of the compensation teachers enjoy. School districts offer valuable fringe benefits worth thousands of dollars. Although some differences exist among districts with regard to the exact amount and type of benefits provided, the items listed below provide a rough idea of what you can expect to receive.

Sick leave. Ten days are average, with unused sick leave accumulating throughout your teaching career.

Personal business leave/sabbaticals. One to three days per calendar year for emergency personal absences are typical. Sabbatical leaves are for independent study and research, professional improvement, or travel; they last for several months and are only available to experienced teachers. Other benefits along these lines might include maternity, military or other special leaves.

Professional leave. School boards frequently allow teachers (with prior approval) to attend educational conferences, seminars, and workshops.

Insurance. The extensive array of available insurance includes programs for health, dental, vision, life, disability, and liability coverage; some of these programs are free to the teacher, while others involve a joint contribution between the school district and the teacher.

Paid vacations and holidays. For a breakdown of these benefits, see the following section, which provides a sample calendar breakdown of common paid vacation time (specifically, winter and spring breaks).

It's also a good idea to have a strong "feel" for such issues as promotions policies and the initial probationary period of a new hire. Of course, these are questions that should have been addressed during the hiring process, but it's a good idea to keep written records (where possible) of such items to avoid any ambiguity.

Working Conditions:
Daily and Yearly Schedules

Teachers work approximately 35 hours a week. You will spend additional time at home grading papers, writing lesson plans, creating room displays, and so on. A duty-free lunch and/or professional preparation period is provided each work day. Class size, or student-teacher ratio, depends upon your subject area and grade level; expect to teach between 18 and 30 students during the school day.

Sample Elementary Teacher's Schedule

8:30 a.m.	Sign-in
8:50 - 9:00	Students arrive
9:00 - 12:00	Morning instruction
12:00 - 12:30 p.m.	Lunch
12:30 - 1:00	Playground supervision
1:00 - 3:00	Afternoon instruction
3:00	Students dismissed
3:00 - 3:30	Preparation period
3:30	Sign-out

Sample High School Teacher's Schedule

8:00 a.m.	Sign-in
8:15 - 8:30	Homeroom
8:34 - 9:14	First period class
9:18 - 9:58	Second period class
10:02 - 10:42	Third period class
10:46 - 11:26	Preparation (fourth period)
11:30 - 12:10 p.m.	Lunch (fifth period)
12:14 - 12:54	Sixth period class
12:58 - 1:38	Hall duty (seventh period)
1:42 - 2:22	Eighth period class
2:26 - 3:00	Supervised activities
3:00	Sign-out

There is no "typical" school year, as schedules vary from district to district, but a broad outline of what you might expect is possible to construct.

As a new teacher, you might be required to report at the end of August for in-service training -- students usually report after Labor Day. For the first semester, holidays would be Veteran's day, Thanksgiving, the "winter break" around Christmas and Hanukkah, New Year's Day, and Martin Luther King, Jr., Day. Pupil progress reports would fall due in November and January.

The second semester customarily runs from January to June. Holidays celebrated during this period include President's Day, the spring break period, and Memorial Day. Pupil progress reports would fall due in April and June. During this period, you should count on at least two "professional days" -- time that you are not actually spending with students, but rather on administrative or departmental matters.

Each semester is usually structured to allow approximately 90 teaching days.

What Do Teachers REALLY Do?

Before you enter into the demanding and sometimes hectic world of the daily classroom environment, it's probably a good idea to review a few "fundamentals" -- some basic points that will remind you of the fact that your *real* job description transcends your daily schedule on a regular basis. Even if you are returning to the classroom after only a short absence, review the points below to ensure that, on the issues that matter most, you are in control of your surroundings -- and not the other way around!

Teachers...	develop daily, written lesson plans.
Teachers...	use testing instruments to assess students' academic needs.
Teachers...	assist in insuring excellent student attendance.
Teachers...	observe students' peer relationships.
Teachers...	participate regularly in after-school activities and parent conferences.
Teachers...	conduct themselves in a professional manner at all times.
Teachers...	guide students in practice areas.
Teachers...	respond promptly to administrative requests.
Teachers...	are enthusiastic about the process of learning.
Teachers...	fill in for other faculty members upon request by school administrators.
Teachers...	encourage proper social habits in their students.
Teachers...	anticipate and plan for individual differences among students.
Teachers...	offer a variety of learning situations.
Teachers...	refer students who show evidence of special learning problems or disabilities to the appropriate programs.
Teachers...	are open to new ideas and new teaching techniques.
Teachers...	show sound judgment, poise, and tact throughout the school day.
Teachers...	write long-range units of instruction.
Teachers...	inform students of their academic progress.
Teachers...	maintain school safety standards.
Teachers...	keep accurate attendance records and other documents as required by law.
Teachers...	see that classrooms are well-ventilated and well-lighted.
Teachers...	modify instruction to meet the unique needs of students.
Teachers...	establish routines that facilitate learning.

Teachers...	monitor student progress by constructing and administering tests, correcting and grading all class assignments, and keeping records of all work.
Teachers...	use a wide variety of instructional materials.
Teachers...	expect their students to achieve.
Teachers...	work harmoniously with other staff members in providing the fullest educational opportunities to students.
Teachers...	understand the physical, intellectual, social, and emotional growth patterns of children.
Teachers...	appeal to students' higher level critical thinking skills.
Teachers...	develop learning activities out of student interests.
Teachers...	keep parents informed of students' progress and behavior on a regular basis.
Teachers...	report potential health problems to parents and school officials.
Teachers...	display high written and oral communication skills.
Teachers...	instruct in accordance with approved curriculum.
Teachers...	motivate students to achieve.
Teachers...	demonstrate excellence in their subject area(s).
Teachers...	maintain student files and parental correspondence in a confidential manner.
Teachers...	serve on a variety of faculty committees.
Teachers...	keep in good order all classroom equipment and supplies.
Teachers...	communicate the purpose of each lesson they teach.
Teachers...	structure lessons so that students succeed.
Teachers...	answer students' questions clearly and knowledgeably.
Teachers...	are prepared to offer remedial or advanced instruction depending upon individual needs.
Teachers...	continue their own education.
Teachers...	incorporate recommendations and suggestions from conferences and special meetings into their curriculum.
Teachers...	relate instruction to predetermined objectives.
Teachers...	assist students on an individual and group basis.
Teachers...	use grammatically correct English in the classroom.
Teachers...	cooperate with school administrators in promoting effective learning.
Teachers...	provide for and encourage student participation.
Teachers...	are responsible for the overall discipline of their students.
Teachers...	evaluate the performance of classroom aides.
Teachers...	promote students' self-discipline.
Teachers...	create and maintain an attractive classroom environment conducive to learning.
Teachers...	display current bulletin boards with examples of student work.
Teachers...	*DO MORE!*

CHAPTER SUMMARY

Teaching contracts are used in small- and medium-sized school districts; large urban districts follow agreements negotiated by local school boards and teacher unions.

Carefully study any contract for employment; be certain you can fulfill all of its provisions before signing.

Teachers' pay, historically low, has started to show signs of definite improvement.

Obtaining one or more advanced degrees is the best long-term strategy for increasing your pay.

There is an extensive package of fringe benefits available to teachers.

Teachers perform a multitude of tasks in and out of the classroom.

Teachers work an average of 35 hours per week and 180 days per school year.

Six:
Additional
Opportunities
In Teaching

Other Roads to Travel

After securing your initial teaching position, you should maintain a broad career perspective that takes advantage of the many new and challenging horizons available outside the local classroom.

Your developing teaching skills and academic expertise can be both marketable and profitable in a wide variety of settings. Opportunities abound for educators in foreign countries, in thousands of private schools, and in college campuses throughout the country. Independent tutoring, fellowships and grants, and curriculum writing programs are other areas that the creative and informed teacher needs to investigate.

It's your life -- it's your career. Be creative!

Overseas Teaching

The Mutual Educational and Cultural Exchange Act of 1961 authorizes the international educational and cultural exchange program known as the Fulbright Program. Elementary and secondary school teachers, college and university instructors, and assistant professors are eligible to apply for a foreign teaching position under the auspices of this program. Forty-three countries have established binational educational commissions or foundations to assist in its administration. An applicant must be a U.S. citizen, hold at least a Bachelor's degree, possess three years of full-time teaching experience, and be currently employed in the subject field at the appropriate level of the position for which the application is submitted.

Under the Fulbright program, teaching arrangements are of two types -- direct exchange and one-way placement. In direct exchange (or "interchange"), foreign teachers are referred by the educational foundations in their own countries. With the approval of American school officials, the foreign teachers then exchange positions with American teachers. (American teachers must also receive approval from their respective administrators).

In addition to this well-known program, there are a multitude of seminars and workshops offered abroad -- items of interest to teachers, school administrators, and curriculum specialists. Instructors teach an American public school curriculum to American students living overseas. Salaries are comparable to those in the United States. Housing, or a tax-free cost of living allowance, is also provided.

The primary purpose of these exchange programs is to broaden the participant's understanding of another culture and to share those perspectives gained by cross-cultural experiences with students, colleagues, and community members.

Hundreds of overseas schools (pre-kindergarten through high school) are constantly seeking qualified American teachers. Generally, these schools can be grouped into four distinct categories:

Private American and international schools. These institutions are assisted by the U.S. Department of State. The ability to speak a foreign language is seldom required because the curriculum is based upon American scholastic requirements. Typically, students are children of ambassadors, consul employees, or personnel from major international corporations who are preparing to qualify for admission to an American or European university.

Military educational institutions. The Department of Defense operates 300 schools located in 27 countries with a total school enrollment of 170,000 American students. Teachers in these schools are U.S. Government employees and comprise a staff similar to those of public schools in the United States including special and vocational educators.

Humanitarian or charitable organizations. A rewarding professional experience may also be gained through teaching in Third World countries with church-affiliated schools or with the Peace Corps, which offers teaching opportunities in 61 countries in Africa, Asia, and Latin America. Although the salary might be low and living conditions inadequate by American standards, the sense of fulfillment and job satisfaction far outweighs these discomforts. The ability to speak a foreign language (or a ready willingness to learn) is a prime consideration here.

International locations of U.S.-based firms. Major United States corporations with international offices have a need for teachers to instruct the children of their employees. Investment firms and oil corporations, for example, have substantial numbers of personnel (with dependents) located in foreign countries. Salaries in schools designed to meet the requirements of these employees are usually higher than average, but you must be prepared to accept an assignment wherever an opening occurs -- including remote areas. Candidates should contact the company headquarters directly for information regarding particular sites and qualifications.

Before getting your passport and packing your new luggage for adventurous and exotic classrooms, take a moment to reflect upon the necessary qualifications and personal attributes of overseas teaching. You must be certified to teach in one of the 50 states; possess an advanced degree or have completed substantial graduate work; and be able to show evidence of several years of previous successful teaching experience (the exact requirements may vary from program to program). In addition, fluency in a foreign language is suggested.

In addition, you should be in good health (a physical examination is required) and maintain the emotional maturity and professional resourcefulness necessary when working in another country. Avoiding "culture shock" often requires creativity and a certain degree of inner strength, as well as tolerance and respect for greatly divergent political systems and individual lifestyles.

Preference for overseas positions is usually given to single teachers and teaching couples without dependents, due to limited housing and the high cost of transportation.

Still interested? On the following page you'll find a list of important addresses that will aid in your quest for a foreign teaching assignment, followed by a brief listing of placement services and overseas recruitment fairs. (These resources are frequently utilized by educators desiring foreign teaching positions. Registration fees and other charges may be assessed; you should also be prepared for an interview.) Finally, in compiling your own research, remember that the library is also a viable source for directories of international schools and firms operating in foreign countries. Letters can be addressed to the appropriate headmaster or superintendent; be sure to include complete college transcripts, resume, verification of state certification, and letters of recommendation. Always request information with an eye to the calendar; leave ample time to send in your application for the subsequent school year.

Resources: Overseas Employment

Fulbright Program

Office of International
Education
U.S. Department of Education
Washington DC 20036

(Request a copy of the
publication entitled
"Agencies Administering
Fulbright Programs in
Cooperation with the
International Com-
munication Agency
and the Board of
Foreign Scholarships")

Teaching Seminars

Council for International
  Exchange of Scholars
11 Dupont Circle NW
Suite 300
Washington DC 20036

*University Lecturing and
  Advanced Research*

Institute of International
  Education
809 United Nations Plaza
New York, New York 10017

*Private and International
  Schools*

Office of Overseas Schools
(A/OS)
Room 234, SA-6
U.S. Department of State
Washington, DC 20520

(Request a copy of the
publication entitled
"Overseas American --
Sponsored Elementary and
Secondary Schools Assisted
by the U.S. Department
of State")

*American Military Dependent's
  Schools*

U.S. Department of Defense
Office of Dependent Schools
Room 152
Hoffman Building #1
2461 Eisenhower Avenue
Alexandria, Virginia 22331

(Request a copy of the
publication entitled
"Overseas Employment for
Educators")

*Humanitarian and Church-
  Affiliated Groups*

United Church Board for
  World Ministries
475 Riverside Drive
New York, New York 10115

The Peace Corps
800-424-8580, extension 30

*Placement Services and
  Overseas Recruitment Fairs*

Overseas Placement Service
  For Educators
University of Northern Iowa
Room 152, Gilchrist Hall
Cedar Falls, Iowa 50614

Educational Career Services
UCLA
405 Hilgard Avenue
Los Angeles, California 90024

International Schools Service
P.O. Box 5910
Princeton, New Jersey 08540

Teacher Overseas Recruiting
Centers
P.O. Box 9027
Cleveland, Ohio 44109

Private Schools

Recent years have witnessed an upsurge in the popularity of private education; according to the National Center for Educational Statistics, more than five million students are currently enrolled in private elementary and secondary schools. Private institutions employ hundreds of thousands of teachers and offer many significant career opportunities to the beginning instructor.

How do you enter this segment of the education field? There are several steps you must follow.

First, choose the type of private school that best suits your training and background. Day care centers, religious-affiliated schools, non-sectarian independent schools, and college preparatory boarding schools are just a few of the options available. Also, remember that there are private institutions of learning at both the elementary and secondary or high school level.

Next, gather your sources of information. As we've seen, contacts within your community, as well as your college placement office, can provide invaluable leads. If you live in a rural or small-town area, purchase a newspaper of a larger metropolitan area. Classified ads under "Education" can be an abundant source of leads for private academies, military schools, and college prep schools. The yellow pages of large cities also contain a listing of "Private Schools" -- providing you with ready access to addresses and telephone numbers. In short, finding a job in private education is quite similar to the process you'd employ in examining employment prospects in public education. Virtually all the potential resources discussed earlier are still applicable here.

Review your qualifications before applying and you'll maximize your chances for acceptance. Most private institutions require state certification or issue their own "professional certificate" based upon your training, credentials, and experience. Generally, salary and employee benefits are not as extensive in private schools as they are in large, urban school districts. Formal contracts for both full- and part-time positions are a condition of employment in private schools.

College and University Teaching

Traditionally, there has been more competition for teaching jobs at the college level than at the elementary or secondary level. An oversupply of qualified applicants, when combined with declining college enrollments, could often result in hundreds of candidates applying for a single assistant professorship. Today, however, a new trend is emerging -- researchers predict a sharp upswing in college faculty hiring by the mid-1990's. Increased enrollments (particularly among adult students) coupled with extensive retirements of current professors, has given rise to optimism for those teachers contemplating careers in higher education.

There are numerous benefits to teaching at the college level, including: higher starting salaries; modern research facilities; travel allowances; flexible schedules; the possibility of tenure; corporate and government consulting contracts; and the general level of prestige associated with higher education.

If you do decide to enter this field (which is, make no mistake, still fiercely competitive at the upper levels), lay the groundwork well ahead of time. Public and private school teachers who have long-range goals of securing positions in higher education must plan now for their move up the academic ladder. It is true that forecasts indicate more and more opportunities will become available for teachers with a master's degree or doctorate who wish to enter the realm of higher academia. But don't limit your horizons strictly to classroom instruction and research. Administrative positions such as counselors, deans, provosts, and curriculum specialists will also be needed.

College faculty and administrators within your graduate department can provide the most current information about employment trends of recent graduates. College professors have their own networking system and frequently keep their students aware of vacancies at local universities as they become available.

Professional organizations conduct surveys and publish information about the college job market. Maintain an active membership in professional organizations to receive their mailings. Visit a university library on a regular basis; some widely circulated national publications for higher education job announcements are: *The Chronicle of Higher*

Education, the *Affirmative Action Register,* and the *American Psychological Association Monitor.*

An "underground job market" can sometimes be of more assistance than published vacancies. Besides contacting your professors, attend professional association conventions to meet with university hiring officials. Review association journals and newsletters -- pay close attention to announcements of retirements, promotions, sabbaticals, and special government projects. All of these natural occurrences provide for new faculty openings.

Keeping your credentials file up-to-date is vital in the college job market. Record all seminars and workshops you may attend; include fellowships and other honors and awards you receive -- even if it necessitates the expense of revising your resume on a monthly basis.

Submit letters of inquiry according to a periodic schedule. Although there may not exist any current openings on a staff, search and screening committees need your supporting documents on file for easy access when a vacancy does occur in your field.

Respond promptly to the screening committee's request for additional information that will bolster your candidacy.

Be certain that at least one of your letters of recommendation is from a current college or university staff member. As a safety measure, check back with the appropriate university placement officials and verify that your credentials file has been received and your application is being processed.

Don't neglect jobs in local junior or community colleges, including part-time work. These positions require a minimum of a master's degree in the area of specialization, and some advanced graduate or doctoral study is usually preferred. Remember, part-time jobs can lead to full-time ones; junior college teaching success can lead to college and university teaching success.

Tutoring

How many times have parents or colleagues admired your rapport with students? Or praised your creative teaching style? Or admired your ability to transform difficult concepts into easily understandable lessons? These skills can mean extra money if you can translate them into tutoring hours. Tutors work in a variety of work settings, including after-school sessions, private services, or freelancing.

A brief analysis of each of these areas follows.

School-based tutoring. Depending upon the availability of funds for extracurricular pay, there's a good chance you can supplement your base salary without leaving your classroom. Tutoring programs are usually scheduled for after school, but if you are willing to forego a preparation period within the school day, you can probably qualify for overtime pay. Discuss with your principal the idea of initiating a tutorial program. (Of course, it's easier to approach your principal once you have built a solid reputation as a teacher who excels with remedial or gifted students.) If funds are not available at your school, inquire at the district office regarding student tutoring programs.

Private Tutoring Services. Parents frequently utilize the services of privately-owned outside companies to improve their children's reading and math abilities. Besides working in these basic school subject areas, tutoring companies also prepare students for specific examinations such as the ACT, GRE, PSAT, and SAT. Full- and part-time job opportunities for energetic teachers abound in this area. Some tutoring companies have been started by former teachers -- and hire teachers exclusively. National firms have developed franchise chains of after-school learning centers and are actively seeking teachers to assist in their operation. These centers have hours that are easily adaptable to a teacher's schedule -- usually from 3:00 to 8:00 p.m. on weekdays and from 9:00 to 5:00 p.m. on Saturdays. Pay for teacher-tutors ranges from $6.00 to $10.00 per hour. Consult your local newspaper's help wanted section to find current tutoring jobs. You should also check your local telephone directory's classified section under "Schools" for a comprehensive listing of private tutoring companies in your area.

Freelance tutoring. Perhaps you have a special talent in music or art, or have graduate training in a particular field. Capitalize on your talents and you can develop your own independent tutoring service. Mention to colleagues and parents that you tutor students after school for a nominal fee; place small ads in your local newspaper; have business cards printed and distribute them whenever and wherever you feel it's appropriate. You may be surprised at the number of referrals you'll generate.

Some types of tutoring are more often in demand than others. These popular areas include lessons in: voice, singing and musical instruments; painting and drawing; remedial reading and math; advanced subjects such as physics and calculus; test-taking skills; and general development of good study habits. You may decide to team up with one or two of your colleagues and expand the subjects offered. Most tutoring sessions last for one hour once or twice a week; the number of students you instruct depends primarily upon your availability. Many teachers who freelance in this way employ a sliding scale fee structure; that is, they adjust their rates according to the income of the student's family.

Still More Opportunities...

Examination proctors. Personnel departments of cities and national examination services need proctors to administer a multitude of tests. Teachers are naturals for this part-time work (most exams are given during evening hours or on Saturdays) because of their familiarity with testing instruments and procedures. Exam proctors earn from $25.00 to $75.00 per test. Contact your city government or one of the national testing services for detailed information on how to become an examination proctor.

Fellowships, grants, and independent studies. Teachers welcome the summer for individual enrichment. Workshops, seminars, and grants provide instructors with the luxury of studying and researching while getting paid at the same time. Carefully read all your school's bulletins beginning in January to watch for announcements of summer opportunities for teachers. Openings are limited and fill up quickly. Act promptly to submit the required paperwork well in advance of deadline dates.

In addition to workshops and seminars, the federal government sponsors summer programs for teachers. Two sources to contact for publications and applications are The National Endowment for the Arts (for teachers of music, art, and literature), and the National Endowment for the Humanities (for teachers of history, English, and political science). While each endowment maintains separate offices, the mailing address for both is:

1100 Pennsylvania Avenue, NW
Washington, DC 20506

State Departments of Education. These bodies have a need for certified teachers to evaluate textbooks and other curriculum. Inquire at your Department of Education or Department of Public Instruction for news of upcoming projects, surveys, pilot programs, and teacher writing assignments. Teachers who serve on these committees are compensated on an hourly or per diem basis.

Textbook Writing and Educational Sales. If you have a talent for educational writing or public speaking, contact the textbook publishers in your area. Writing and conducting sales presentations for these firms can be done on a freelance basis that is adaptable to your regular teaching schedule. The salary for freelance writing is usually on an hourly basis; compensation for sales work is based on commissions, with travel expenses reimbursed.

CHAPTER SUMMARY

Classroom teaching gives rise to a multitude of related full- and part-time jobs.

Teaching in a foreign country is a distinct possibility for an experienced instructor with advanced degrees.

There are thousands of overseas teaching positions offered by the federal government and large American corporations.

Private elementary and secondary schools enroll millions of students and offer career opportunities to thousands of teachers.

Finding faculty positions at the college or university level is becoming a more realistic goal due to demographic changes.

After-school student tutoring programs are rapidly expanding throughout the U.S; teachers can work for a franchise chain or do independent, freelance tutoring.

Work also exists for teachers who wish to be examination proctors, participate in summer fellowships or grant programs, serve on textbook committees, write educational curriculum, or sell educational products.

INDEX